T0046814

An
Angel
for
Any
thing

© Jason Fell Photography

About the Author

Richard Webster was born and raised in New Zealand. He has been interested in the psychic world since he was nine years old. He became interested in angels in his mid-twenties when he started receiving messages from his guardian angel. Richard's first book was published in 1972, fulfilling a childhood dream of becoming an author. Richard is now the author of more than a hundred books and is still writing today. His best-selling books include *Spirit Guides & Angel Guardians* and *The Secret to Attracting Luck*. Richard has appeared on many radio and TV programs in the United States and abroad. He travels widely every year, lecturing and conducting workshops around the world. He and his wife live in New Zealand and have three children and five grandchildren.

An Angel for Anything

INVOKE ANGELIC ALLIES TO ELEVATE YOUR LIFE

RICHARD WEBSTER

Llewellyn Publications • Woodbury, Minnesota

An Angel for Anything: Invoke Angelic Allies to Elevate Your Life Copyright ©
2024 by Richard Webster. All rights reserved. No part of this book may be used or
reproduced in any manner whatsoever, including internet usage, without written
permission from Llewellyn Worldwide Ltd., except in the case of brief quotations
embodied in critical articles and reviews.

FIRST EDITION
First Printing, 2024

Cover design by Shannon McKuhen

Llewellyn Publications is a registered trademark of Llewellyn Worldwide Ltd.

Library of Congress Cataloging-in-Publication Data (Pending)
ISBN: 978-0-7387-7571-5

Llewellyn Worldwide Ltd. does not participate in, endorse, or have any authority or
responsibility concerning private business transactions between our authors and the
public.

All mail addressed to the author is forwarded but the publisher cannot, unless specifically instructed by the author, give out an address or phone number.

Any internet references contained in this work are current at publication time,
but the publisher cannot guarantee that a specific location will continue to be maintained. Please refer to the publisher's website for links to authors' websites and other
sources.

Llewellyn Publications
A Division of Llewellyn Worldwide Ltd.
2143 Wooddale Drive
Woodbury, MN 55125-2989
www.llewellyn.com

Printed in the United States of America

Other Books by Richard Webster
Published by Llewellyn

Guardian Angels

Archangels

The Secret to Attracting Luck

How to Use a Pendulum

How to Use a Crystal

Angels for Beginners

Note

All quotes from the Bible are from the King James version.

Dedication

For my good friend and fellow angel communicator,
Dr. Jeremy Weiss.

Acknowledgments

I owe a huge debt of gratitude to all the staff of Llewellyn Publications who have guided and helped me over the last thirty years. The enthusiasm, friendliness, encouragement, and support from everyone has been incredible. For this book, I'd especially like to thank Laura Kurtz, Amy Glaser, Bill Krause, and Oxana Schroeder.

I have many friends around the world who have helped me develop my passion for angels. I'd especially like to thank Pablo Amira, Nick Belleas, Doug Dyment, Tony Iacoviello, Jesse James, Kenton Knepper, Sandi Liss, Robyn Luke, Darrell Mac, Mick Peck, Ken Ring, Blair Robertson, Neal Scryer, Jon Stetson, Luca Volpe, Alan Watson, and Dr. Jeremy Weiss.

I'd also like to thank my wife, Margaret, and our three children, Nigel, Charlotte, and Philip, for their love and constant encouragement. I'll never forget the day when Nigel, aged about twelve at the time, said, "Dad is writing a book." It was true. We were having a family lunch, but I was immersed in whatever I was writing at the time. It was a lesson learned, and I hope I'm better now at not writing at mealtimes.

Finally, thank you for buying this book.

Contents

Introduction 1

Chapter One
The Angelic Kingdom 5

Chapter Two
How to Communicate with Angels 9

Chapter Three
How to Contact a Particular Angel 39

Chapter Four
The Angels of Spirituality 61

Chapter Five
How to Work with Archangel Michael 69

Chapter Six
How to Work with Archangel Raphael 85

Chapter Seven
How to Work with Archangel Gabriel 93

Chapter Eight
How to Work with Archangel Uriel 99

Chapter Nine
How to Work with Archangel Metatron 107

Chapter Ten
How to Love Others and Yourself 115

Chapter Eleven
How to Find Your Purpose in Life 125

Chapter Twelve
How to Work with the Angels of Forgiveness 133

Chapter Thirteen

How to Work with the Angels of Kindness   141

Chapter Fourteen

How to Work with the Angels of Mindfulness   149

Chapter Fifteen

How to Work with the Angels of Encouragement   159

Chapter Sixteen

How to Work with the Angels of Abundance   167

Conclusion   189

Appendix   191

Bibliography   205

Introduction

Angels can appear in a limitless range of shapes, sizes, and colors. They also have specific roles and tasks to perform. If you need comfort in a moment of despair, you might find that an angel who specializes in helping people in difficult situations will provide you with the necessary support and assistance to help ease your pain.

If you're doing some serious study, and need help, there are many angels who'd be delighted to provide support and help. Many angels provide motivation and encouragement, and they enjoy helping you experience the joys of success and accomplishment once you've succeeded. The angels of healing are ready to help everyone who asks for assistance. You can use the techniques in this book to communicate with any angel you wish to ask for help in achieving any positive purpose you have in mind.

About three years ago, I was asked an interesting question after I'd given a talk on angels. A lady in the audience said that she'd reached the age of fifty-seven without needing an angel. Why would she want to invite angels into her life? I explained that angels are always present to provide support, guidance, and love. Every life has its share of good and bad times, and the bad times are always difficult, especially so when we're trying to do everything on our own. The painful times

1

can be made easier and the good times even more joyful when shared with angels.

"I'm an artist," she said. "Could the angels help me be more creative? Or make more money?"

I wasn't sure if she was being serious or facetious but hoped they were genuine questions. "There are angels who specialize in enhancing creativity," I said "And there are angels who help people achieve abundance. All of them would be only too happy to help you. All you have to do is ask."

She didn't look convinced but said she'd give it a try and see what happened.

More than two years later, I was invited to speak at a spiritual center about fifty miles from my home. When I arrived, the person who greeted me was the lady who'd asked me the question. I'd been booked by the center on her recommendation, as she wanted to let me know how well she was doing as an artist and a businesswoman after including angels in her life. When she introduced me, she told everyone that she now knows why we should all invite angels into our lives.

I was fascinated, partly because the occasion when I met her was one of the last live talks I gave before COVID spread around the world, and the talk where I met her again was the first live talk I gave once life started to get back to normal. I was also delighted that she was communicating with angels, as I didn't think she would. Finally, I was impressed that her art business had taken off and that she had thrived during a time when the economy was terrible.

The main reason to invite angels into your life is because you'll immediately gain angelic help in everything you do. The angels will provide you with guidance, help, encouragement, and advice for any task whenever you need it. They'll never interfere but know exactly what you need at any moment, and they're willing to help whenever you ask.

Invoking (summoning) the angels is the first step to enhancing every area of your life, including your spirituality. Once you've done this, you'll feel that you're constantly surrounded with peace, love, kindness, and positivity. Obviously, you'll still experience the ups and downs we all experience in life, but you'll find you can handle the negative periods with greater ease and effectiveness, and you'll experience more positivity all day, every day.

Chapter One

The Angelic Kingdom

About two thousand years ago, religious scholars started classifying the angels into different groups depending on the work they did and their closeness to God. This classification became a hierarchy, with the most important angels who were closest to God at the top of the pyramid, and the lowly "worker bee" angels at the bottom, much like a diagram of a large organization, with the CEO at the top and the most junior employees at the lowermost level. The earliest known Christian account of an angelic hierarchy is in the *Testament of Adam*, which was probably written before 400 CE. None of this means anything to the angels, as they all know what their duties and tasks are and spend their time performing them.

The best-known grouping of angels was the hierarchy of angels devised by an anonymous scholar in the fifth century CE named Pseudo-Dionysius. He was probably a Syrian monk who called himself Dionysius possibly because he wanted his writings to be credited to Dionysius the Areopagite, who was briefly mentioned in the Bible (Acts 17:34). The real Dionysius later became the first bishop of Athens and a Christian martyr. Pseudo-Dionysius classified the angels into three triads, or levels. Each triad contained three ranks of angels.

Triad One:
The Angels Closest to God

Seraphim

The word "seraphim" comes from the Hebrew *sarap,* which means "burning one." The seraphim are angels of fire and light who can purify people with a flash of lightning.

Cherubim

The word "cherubim" come from *kerub*, a Hebrew word that means "fullness of knowledge." The cherubim look after the sun, moon, and stars. They also keep the heavenly records and help people (and lower orders of angels) gain knowledge and spiritual wisdom.

Thrones

The Thrones are sometimes called "Wheels," as the prophet Ezekiel saw them as fiery wheels full of eyes. They are the angels of justice and advise God when he has to make important decisions.

Triad Two:
The Princes or Leaders of the Heavenly Kingdom

Dominions or Dominations

The Dominions are usually considered the oldest order of angels. They supervise the lower ranks of angels and issue the orders that ensure the universe works as it should. Although they are extremely powerful angels, they're also angels of mercy.

Virtues

The Virtues carry out the instructions of the Dominions and look after all the natural laws of the universe. They help people who need courage and the ability to relate well with others.

Powers

The Powers look after the Akashic Records and protect people's souls. They are highly courageous and prevent evil spirits from trying to overthrow the world. One of their tasks is to guard the entrances to heaven.

Triad Three:
The Ministering Angels

Principalities

The principalities supervise and protect countries, cities, towns, and sacred sites. They are good administrators who are actively involved in governing the universe. One of their most important tasks is to encourage and help guardian angels in their work.

Archangels

The word "archangel" means "chief messenger." Only three angels were referred to by name in the Bible: Michael, Gabriel, and Lucifer. Of these, Michael is the only one ever called an archangel in the Bible (Jude 9). However, for almost two thousand years, people have thought that the seven angels who stood before God in the book of Revelation (8:2) were all archangels. These angels are Michael, Gabriel, Raphael, Uriel, Raguel, Sariel, and Remiel. The first four of these are called the Four Angels of the Presence.

Angels

The angels in this group could be considered privates (or the lowest rank) in God's army, but this doesn't make them any less important than other angels. In fact, as far as human beings are concerned, they're extremely valuable, as these are the ones people most often see. Because everything in the universe is looked after by an angel, this rank of angels is larger than any other group, and most work as God's messengers.

The members of this choir include the angels of joy, love, hope, courage, knowledge, faith, and peace, and they can help you with an unlimited number of concerns.

Guardian angels also belong to this rank. Everyone has at least one guardian angel. Their task is to look after a specific human being from the moment they're born until the end of their life. Some people believe that guardian angels start looking after their charges from the moment of conception to remain with them during all of their incarnations. Guardian angels provide companionship, protection, and guidance. They encourage good thoughts and deeds and also provide comfort when the people they're looking after are suffering. Although they can offer help, they can't override free will or do anything if their charges choose to ignore their suggestions.

The angels we'll be working with in this book all come from the two lowest groups in the hierarchy of angels: angels and archangels. This doesn't mean that they're less important than other angels. We work with them solely because the angels in these groups are the ones who are most regularly in contact with human beings.

In the next chapter we'll start looking at different approaches to communicate with angels.

Chapter Two

How to Communicate with Angels

You are surrounded by countless angels all the time, and all of them want to work with you. All you have to do is ask. Unfortunately, many people never do this, either knowing nothing about angels or having no interest in the spiritual world.

Other people have a variety of fears that prevent them from making a spiritual connection. They may believe that communicating with angels is somehow irreligious and goes against what they were taught in Sunday school. They may consider themselves to be so insignificant and unimportant that they would be ignored if they tried to communicate with angels. They may have doubts about the existence of angels or think themselves too grown-up to communicate with invisible helpers. Whatever the reason for not connecting with angels, there's no need for us to live our lives without experiencing the joy, love, support, and companionship that these divine messengers want to provide. Luckily, the angels are always nearby, and you can call on them whenever you need help of any sort. The best time is when you're in a quiet, peaceful, meditative state. You might sit down in a comfortable chair, close your eyes, and take slow, deep breaths until you feel relaxed. Once you've reached this peaceful state, ask the angel you wish to speak with to join you.

Lying in bed either before you go to sleep or when you first wake up are also good times to contact the angelic realms. If you enjoy walking, you can enter the desired state while taking a stroll in the countryside or walking beside a stream, river, or lake. Green grass and blue water are both good for your body, mind, and soul.

Experiencing Angels

People experience angels in different ways. Consequently, it's impossible for anyone to tell you how you will experience an angelic visitation. You may have a feeling that an angel is with you. You might feel a gentle touch. You might detect a beautiful scent or perfume, such as roses. It could also happen as a strong emotion or important thoughts that appear in your mind.

Many people want to see the angels they're communicating with. People who are naturally clairvoyant can sometimes see angels using the mind's eye or inner vision rather than with physical sight. Although anyone can see an angel under certain circumstances, it's rare; most people who regularly communicate with angels never actually see them. Angels are nonphysical beings who live on the mental plane, so their bodies are as visible to us as our thoughts.

When we invite angels to join us, we're inviting them into our heads, where their messages usually come as thoughts in our minds. As always, there are exceptions, and everyone is different. Some people can hear angels talking with them, sometimes even in song.

Once you start communicating with an angel, the relationship will grow and develop, and you'll be able to make instant contact whenever you need that particular angel's help. In return, the angel will contact you from time to time and play an increasingly important role in your life. This is always the case once you make contact with your guardian angel, but you can also establish close relationships with any of the angels you decide to work with.

How to Invoke Angels

Invocation is the act of summoning an angel for a beneficial or positive purpose. In Western magic, an invocation usually involves the four great Archangels of the Presence, who are also responsible for the four elements: Raphael (air), Michael (fire), Gabriel (water), and Uriel (earth). The invocation is usually conducted inside a magic circle, a space that has always been considered to be sacred and protected.

Angelic Invocation of Protection

This ritual enables you to surround yourself with angelic protection whenever you need it and can be performed anywhere you wish. I prefer to perform it outdoors, but during the winter months I often have to perform my rituals indoors. Make sure that you won't be disturbed for at least half an hour.

The first step is to construct a magic circle or sacred space approximately eight to twelve feet in diameter. When I'm performing this invocation indoors, I use a circular rug to indicate the circumference of the circle. When working outdoors, I usually mark out the circle with rope, cord, or stones. Instead of creating a physical circle, I sometimes visualize the circle I'm working within. If I think I might need them, I place a table to act as an altar and a straight-backed chair in the middle of the circle.

If possible, enjoy a leisurely bath before the invocation and put on clean, loose-fitting clothes. This separates the invocation from your normal, everyday life. The bath also gives you time to think about the purpose of the invocation while you're relaxing in the warm water.

Once you've constructed the circle, bathed, and put on clean clothes, you're ready to start the invocation.

Stand outside the circle, and smile as you're about to summon the four great Archangels of the Presence: Raphael, Michael, Gabriel, and Uriel. Take a deep breath and, as you exhale, step into the circle. Move to the center and face east.

Close your eyes and visualize Archangel Raphael standing in front of you. It makes no difference how you "see" Archangel Raphael—you might visualize a large, powerful angel with huge wings or see him in the way he is most commonly depicted in art: as a traveler with a staff, water gourd, and a large fish. You might see him as a swirling ball of different colors, or maybe feel his presence in your mind. It doesn't matter what image or impression comes into your mind, as it will be the right one for you. When you sense Raphael is standing in front of you, start talking. I prefer to speak out loud, but you might prefer to talk to him in your mind, especially if other people are nearby. You might say something along the lines of: "Thank you, Archangel Raphael, for your support and protection. I'm grateful to you for being here for me and for your guidance and healing. Thank you."

With your eyes still closed, turn ninety degrees to face south. Visualize Archangel Michael in your mind. I "see" Michael as a tall man wearing chain mail, wielding a sword in one hand and holding a set of scales in the other, with one foot resting on a dragon. This is a composite of the many paintings I've seen of Archangel Michael over the years. Your impression of Michael may be completely different. Whatever it is, it will be right for you. Once you sense Michael's presence, speak to him. You might say: "Thank you, Archangel Michael, for your support and protection. Thank you for giving me courage and strength when I most need it. I am very grateful for everything you do to help me. Thank you."

Turn another ninety degrees to face west. Visualize Archangel Gabriel as clearly as you can. I picture Gabriel as an androgynous figure wearing green and blue robes. The figure holds a lily in one hand to symbolize the purity of the Virgin Mary and a trumpet in the other, the one that will be blown to awaken the dead on Judgment Day. Again, this is a composite of different pictures I've seen of Archangel Gabriel over the years. Speak to Gabriel when you sense a presence. You might say: "Thank you, Archangel Gabriel, for your gentleness and devotion. Thank you for being God's messenger and for all your help and support. I am very grateful. Thank you."

Turn to face north. This time, visualize Archangel Uriel standing in front of you. I see Uriel as a powerful-looking man with dark, curly hair and a brown beard. He carries a scroll in one hand. On the palm of his other hand is a burning flame. Most paintings of Uriel show this flame, as his name means "Flame of God." Naturally, your image of Uriel may be quite different. When you sense his presence, say something along the lines of: "Thank you, Archangel Uriel, for all your help and support. Thank you for giving me fresh insights and ideas. Thank you for forcing me to make changes when I'm reluctant to do them myself. Thank you."

Turn to face Archangel Raphael again. You are now totally surrounded and protected by the four great archangels. Inside this circle of protection, you can conduct any rituals you wish, knowing that you are safe, secure, and loved. You can also invite any angels that you'd like to speak with to join you inside the circle.

When the ritual you're performing is over, face Archangel Raphael again and thank him for his love, help, and protection. Say goodbye, and visualize him fading from view. Repeat this with Archangels Michael, Gabriel, and Uriel.

Once you've completed the invocation, step outside the circle. Eat and drink something to help you become fully grounded again. I eat a handful of nuts and raisins and follow it with a glass of water.

After you've gained experience with this invocation, you'll find that you are able to perform it with your eyes open and can "see" the great archangels and the other angels you invite to join you just as clearly as you did with your eyes closed.

Council of Angels

You can summon a council of angels whenever you need help with a particular problem. Councils meet for consultation and advice, and you can invite as many angels as you wish to join you when you have a council meeting. If you have a particular problem you need help with, you might invite one or two angels to provide you with advice, or you might invite a dozen or more. It depends on the type of help you need. If you want to attract love, you might invite a dozen angels to your council meeting, as you'll want as many ideas and suggestions as possible. If you want to buy a house, for instance, you'd probably ask Archangel Uriel to join you, as he is the archangel of abundance and prosperity. If you're holding your council meeting inside your circle and have performed an Angelic Invocation of Protection, this means you'll be helped by Archangel Uriel twice. Even though he'll be helping to protect your sacred space, he'll be pleased to be invited to your council meeting as well.

You can arrange chairs in a circle for the angels to sit on, or you can simply imagine the scene in your head. It's a good idea to hold your first council meetings by setting out chairs anywhere where you have enough room and privacy. Make sure the room is pleasantly warm. If there's enough room, arrange the chairs in a circle. Otherwise, set the chairs in rows and place your chair in front-facing the other chairs.

Sit down in your chair, think of a few things that you're grateful for, and then think of your intention for the meeting.

Close your eyes, take several slow deep breaths, and then surround yourself with a pure, gold light. Allow the light to gradually grow until it fills the entire room. Ask the angels to join you. In your mind's eye, visualize them arriving and filling up all the other chairs in the room.

Smile at the angels and thank them for joining you. Feel the warmth of their love and send love back to them.

They will already know why you're holding the meeting, but tell them again to give yourself a chance to express your feelings and emotions and share any thoughts on whatever the matter happens to be.

Once you've said everything you want to say, either ask specific questions or ask the angels if they have anything they'd like to say. Listen carefully, as their advice comes directly from the Divine. As this can be a highly emotional process, don't worry if you find yourself crying or expressing your feelings in some other way.

Respond to what you're being told. Ask questions if you need clarification or don't fully understand what you've been told.

Once you've received all the information that you need, thank the angels for their help and advice, and say goodbye. Visualize them leaving, and in your mind, smile and wave goodbye.

Spend a few moments thinking about the experience and knowledge you've gained. When you feel ready, give thanks to the Divine, count slowly from one to five, and open your eyes.

Affirmations

Affirmations are short, powerful, positive statements always phrased in the present tense that enable you to focus your thoughts on a single topic. In effect, they enable you to control your thoughts. They can be created and used for almost any purpose, such as increasing motivation, confidence, and positivity. You can also use them to eliminate bad habits and limiting beliefs, such as smoking, eating unhealthy foods, impatience, and negativity. In addition, affirmations can be a powerful tool to help you contact the angelic realms.

Affirmations are repeated over and over again until they become implanted in your mind and effect positive changes in your life. They can be said silently or out loud, and you can say them anywhere at any time. If you're on your own, you might choose to chant or sing them. I find it helpful to repeat them, placing the emphasis on a different word every time I say the affirmation. The best affirmations are ones that you write yourself, as they relate exactly to your needs.

You may find it helpful to write your affirmations on cards and carry one or two of them with you to read whenever you have a spare moment. Alternatively or in addition, you can place them somewhere where you'll see them several times a day.

Affirmations are a convenient way to contact the angelic realms because repeating them on a regular basis increases your angelic awareness and helps you to get closer to them. The angels will respond to your affirmations, and you'll be able to start communicating with them once you sense their presence around you.

Here are some sample angelic affirmations that you can use or modify:

Angels are guiding and protecting me.

Thank you, angels, for your guidance and love.

I am full of divine love.

Thank you, angels, for all the blessings in my life.

The angels fill me with love and inspiration.

I love talking with my guardian angel.

Angels are always with me.

I am open to angelic guidance.

The angels love me, and help me in everything I do.

Angels protect and guide me.

Angels are always watching over me.

My angels love and support me.

I am always enveloped in angelic love.

My angels fill my life with daily miracles.

Thank you, angels, for walking with me every day.

I am constantly full of angelic energy.

The angels help me attract abundance and love.

I communicate with angels easily and effortlessly.

My angels help me create the life of my dreams.

Angels bless me with joy, love, and laughter.

Visualization

The great artist Michelangelo (1475–1564) was said to have "seen" an angel in a block of marble and carved away enough stone to set the angel free. Isn't it wonderful to know that, just like him, you also possess an unbelievably powerful imagination? The pictures you create in your mind's eye determine your reality. Athletes visualize positive outcomes to help them perform at their best, as do successful people in many other fields. People who use visualization negatively see problems and difficulties that hold them back and limit their lives. You can use your imagination to achieve success, failure, and anything in between. What's important to know is that whatever you visualize, your mind will believe it and work to make it happen.

Visualization is a powerful and enjoyable way to establish a connection with the angelic realms. In effect, it's a guided daydream. All you need do is sit down somewhere where you won't be disturbed and visualize yourself connecting with an angel. If you haven't done anything like this before, focus on your guardian angel and your desire to establish a close connection. In your imagination, you can do anything. You might imagine that you're relaxing in the most beautiful place you've ever seen, sitting beside your guardian angel while enjoying a stimulating conversation. You can ask your guardian angel anything you wish, and the replies you receive will be helpful and exactly what you need. You can talk for as long as you wish, and your angel will always give you a hug when you say goodbye.

This is, of course, a visualization, as you're imagining the situation. Repeat it every day, however, and you'll suddenly find that your visualization has become real—the angels will make it happen. Once you reach that state, you'll be able to contact the angels whenever you wish and won't need to visualize them anymore (unless you would like to).

Angel Altar

At its simplest, an altar is any level surface upon which you can place candles, flowers, crystals, and other spiritual objects. You could even use part of a kitchen table or a shelf as an altar. I used an old card table for many years that worked well. I've also used an old wooden crate with a cupboard door resting on top of it to create a flat surface and a coffee table with a drawer on one side. If you're working outdoors, you might find a suitable flat rock, or even place your altar cloth on the ground. A permanent altar with a solid wood surface is ideal, but you can set up an impromptu altar anywhere you happen to be.

Whatever your altar's material, it needs to be inside your circle of protection, either in the center or at the edge so that you're facing east when working at it if you prefer.

If you use an altar cloth, make sure that it's used for no other purpose and is stored away when not needed. I have a white linen altar cloth that is embroidered at each end. You might like to make your own altar cloth or buy one; altar cloths and altars, for that matter, are readily available online.

You can place anything you wish on your altar. Because you're using it to contact the angelic realms, you should place spiritual objects on your altar relating to this intent. I have a large selection of angel ornaments from which two or three are usually on my altar at any given time. I also display a couple of candles. I usually use white candles but have a selection of different colors that relate to different angels I might want to communicate with.

Along with the candles, I always have a jug of water on one side of my altar as a precautionary measure, just in case something is accidentally set on fire. I've never had an accident of that sort but I like to be prepared.

Also on my altar are celestite and selenite, crystals known to attract angels. (Angelite, green prehnite, and seraphinite work well, too.) I usually place a bowl of flowers on one side of the altar.

Your altar is a sacred space that can be used for any spiritual purpose. If you use it regularly, it will quickly gain an aura of sanctity that puts you in the right frame of mind whenever you stand or sit in front of it. It will become more sacred as time goes by, making it the perfect place to pray, meditate, communicate with angels, or spend a few minutes quieting your mind after a stressful day.

Once you've created an altar, you need to start using it. This can be done simply by lighting a candle or burning some incense. You might place a sacred object or a few flowers on your altar and then pray or meditate in front of it (see chapter 4).

Angel Cards

Readily available at all New Age stores, angel cards provide a useful way to communicate with angels. Most cards contain a keyword that provides healing and guidance by encouraging you to focus on a particular area of life.

Although it's easy and convenient to buy a set of angel cards, it can be even more rewarding to create your own. I made my first deck using a deck of double-blank playing cards bought online. You might prefer to use file cards, business cards, note cards, or small pieces of paper or cardstock.

On each card, write a word or words that relate to a topic that the angels can help you with. Even though my drawing skills are almost non-existent, I decorate the cards with hearts, stars, and angels, using colored pencils and markers for variety. You might be able to illustrate your cards with attractive drawings. I know several people who decorate their cards with pictures cut from old magazines.

Your card deck can have as many cards as you wish. Most people start with a few cards and gradually increase the number as they think of topics they'd like to discuss with the angels. My first deck began with forty cards and over time increased to about sixty.

When making your own deck, include any topic that relates to you and your needs. If you're wanting to improve your health, for instance, you would include several cards that relate to exercise, nutrition, and healthy foods.

Here are some possible words that you might use:

Abundance	Acceptance	Assertiveness
Balance	Beauty	Blessings
Communication	Compassion	Confidence
Courage	Creativity	Self-discipline
Empathy	Energy	Enthusiasm
Exercise	Fairness	Faith
Forgiveness	Freedom	Friendship
Generosity	Gentleness	Gratitude

Growth	Harmony	Healing
Honesty	Hope	Humor
Inner peace	Insight	Inspiration
Intuition	Joy	Light
Love	Meditation	Motivation
Openness	Patience	Peace
Play	Positivity	Power
Purification	Purpose	Relationship
Reliability	Responsibility	Romance
Security	Sensitivity	Spontaneity
Strength	Success	Surrender
Tenderness	Transformation	Trust
Truth	Understanding	Vitality
Wisdom		

The easiest way to use angel cards is to ask your guardian angel to help you pull the card that will be most helpful in the present moment. Mix the cards and spread them facedown in a line across a table. Hold your left hand a few inches above one end of the row of cards and slowly move it over the cards until you feel it is the right time to stop. Pick up the card directly under your hand: this is the card your angel has chosen for you. As you look at it, think about the message on the card and what relevance it has to you at the moment. Set it in a place where you'll see it several times during the day. Each time you notice it, think of the message and thank your guardian angel for selecting the card for you.

You might prefer to pull out three or four cards and give yourself a reading. Slowly mix the cards while thinking of a problem or concern you have. When the time seems right, stop mixing the cards and place them facedown on a table. Turn over the top card and see how it relates to your concern. If necessary, turn over the next card as well. There'll be times when you need further information that you can gain by turning over additional cards. The first card shows the situation, the second card reveals the challenge or obstacle, the third card shows influences on the situation, and the fourth card reveals the outcome.

If you have a friend who's interested in angels, you can choose a card for each other. Mix the cards while asking the angels to help you choose the right card. When you stop mixing the cards, fan them facedown, and pull out a card for your friend. Your friend will then do the same for you. Don't look at the cards until you both have one.

Flowers

It's not surprising that flowers attract angels; they radiate peace, harmony, joy, and love. No wonder we're told to "stop and smell the flowers." Flowers provide an extremely pleasant way to communicate with the angelic realms and have been associated with angels for thousands of years. In addition to bringing joy to the world with their beauty and scent, flowers have also introduced many people to angels.

You can test the close connection flowers and angels have with each other by walking in a flower garden and pausing each time a flower attracts your attention for any reason. Silently talk to the flower, making special mention of your desire to communicate with angels. Smile at the flower and take several slow, deep breaths. Remain quiet and receptive. If nothing happens after a minute or two, silently thank the flower and move on. A response can occur in a number of ways: You might experience a sense of knowing that angels are present, receive an angelic message as a thought in your mind, or feel a gentle touch on your arm, face, or shoulder. Once you receive a response, talk silently to the angel for as long as you wish.

Flowers make a wonderful addition to an altar, and you can select suitable flowers by their colors, perfume, or symbolic associations. Here are some examples:

- Amaryllis is said to attract angels of abundance and prosperity.
- Apple blossom attracts angels of happiness and love.
- Azaleas attract angels of abundance who will help you with your material needs, as well as providing abundance in other areas of life.
- Camellias attract angels of faithfulness, grace, longevity, and love. In China, camellias are considered symbols of health, beauty, and resilience.
- Pink carnations attract angels of gratitude; white carnations attract angels of pleasant memories; yellow carnations attract angels of joy, happiness, and fulfillment.
- Chrysanthemums attract angels of joy, tranquility, and longevity.
- Cyclamens attract angels who help people deal with their feelings, especially long-standing, deeply embedded issues from the past.
- Daffodils attract angels of forgiveness.
- Dahlias attract messenger angels.
- Gardenias enhance spiritual growth. They attract angels of abundance. Gardenias also attract angels who'll remove fears, doubts, and worries.
- Geraniums attract angels of comfort, guidance, and inspiration. They come in a variety of colors, including pink, purple, lilac, red, and white. Rose geraniums attract angels who release stress and attract enduring love.

- Holly attracts angels who create harmony and happiness within the home. These angels help revitalize relationships that are in danger of failing and help people appreciate what they already have.

- As well as helping people find peace of mind, honeysuckle is also said to attract angels who bring messages from the Divine. These angels also help people live in the present moment, forgive others, and let go of pain and hurt from the past.

- Hyacinths attract angels of wisdom, clarity, and serenity. They speak directly to your soul and enhance spiritual awareness.

- Hydrangeas attract angels of protection who will help you repel all negativity and keep you safe from physical harm.

- The blue flowers of hyssop attract angels of cleansing, purification, humility, and innocence.

- Irises attract angels of protection who protect the home as well as its occupants. It also attracts angels who help people who are grieving.

- Jasmine attracts angels of peace, grace, and love. They help you find peace, no matter what's going on in your life. The word "jasmine" comes from Persian and means "gift from God."

- Lavender attracts angels who surround you with blessings and help you in all areas of your life. Tradition says that lavender also attracts fairies.

- Lilacs attract angels of happiness and joy. They help you eliminate negativity and focus on all the positive aspects of life.

- The lily has always been considered an emblem of innocence and purity. Consequently, it's not surprising that many Renaissance paintings of Archangel Gabriel—especially those depicting the Annunciation when he told the Virgin Mary that she would give birth to Jesus—show him holding a lily to symbolize Mary's purity. Lilies relate to the Holy Spirit and encourage communication with people on the Other Side. Lilies also attract angels of prosperity and abundance.

- Marigolds attract angels of happiness, joy, loyalty, positivity, and longevity. The marigold gained its name ("Marygold") from the Virgin Mary, as it is often associated with her purity and perfection.

- Morning glories attract angels of peace and happiness.

- Pansies attract angels of love who help you express your loving thoughts to all forms of life. Pansies are sometimes called "heartsease," which means *loving remembrance*.

- Roses symbolize perfection and completion. They also attract angels of love and spiritual devotion. Red roses attract angels of passion and romance, white roses attract angels of healing and purification, pink roses attract angels of playfulness and romantic love, and yellow roses attract angels who keep you grounded and safe.

- Tulips attract healing angels. Tulips are also useful for attracting your guardian angel.

Meditation

Meditation has been practiced for thousands of years. In 1928, a 4,000-year-old steatite (soapstone) seal was discovered during an excavation of the ruins of the ancient city of Mohenjo-daro in the

Indus Valley (in modern-day Pakistan) depicting someone sitting on a dais while meditating in the lotus position with their legs crossed.[1]

Meditation is a technique to clear the mind, center yourself, and become one with all life and the world you live in. With meditation, you can control and limit your thoughts and experience your true feelings. The most common way of meditating is focusing on your breathing or the flame of a flickering candle. Meditation is a skill that anyone can learn. Over time and with practice, you'll experience the oneness of the universe, often called cosmic awareness.

Although seated meditation is the most common, you can meditate in many different ways: while walking, running, preparing a meal, eating, washing dishes, or even when you become lost in a pleasurable activity. Mindfulness itself is considered a form of meditation, so it is possible to reach the desired state of calm at almost any time you wish. Meditation eliminates outside distractions and enables you to contact your inner self or subconscious mind. If you ever find yourself daydreaming, you're already an accomplished meditator!

People meditate for many reasons. Health is an important one, as your metabolism, heart rate, and breathing all slow down when you're in a meditative state. Your brain waves move from the conscious state of beta to the more peaceful alpha. Reaching the alpha state reduces stress, anxiety, and blood pressure, and it enables you to gain a calm and peaceful mind. Many people meditate for spiritual growth. Meditation plays an important role in many religions, including Buddhism, Hinduism, Judaism, Sufism, and the Christian mystical tradition.

It can be a good practice to begin and end your day with meditation. A short meditation first thing in the morning and again last

---

1. Leonard George, *Alternative Realities: The Paranormal, the Mystic and the Transcendent in Human Experience* (New York: Facts on File, 1995), 170–71.

thing at night is extremely beneficial. The morning meditation will give you insights about the opportunities in the coming day, and the evening meditation will quieten the mind, enhance inner peace, and create better sleep.

Exercise: Five-Minute Meditation

If you haven't meditated before, start by setting aside five minutes for meditation. As you gain experience, you'll find the length of time you allow will gradually increase. All you need is a quiet space. Here is a simple meditation that will help you gain control of your mind.

Make sure the room you're planning to meditate in is pleasantly warm and that you're wearing loose-fitting clothes. If possible, dim the lights. Sit or lie down and make yourself as comfortable as you can. If you're feeling tired, it's better to sit down; although you will relax, you still want to stay awake during the meditation. Choose a straight-backed chair to ensure no undue pressure is put on any part of your body. Use the back support only if necessary. Ideally, your spine should be as straight as possible. As you need to be comfortable, sit on a cushion and place another one behind your back if needed. If you prefer to lie down on the floor or a recliner, lie on your back with your arms and legs slightly apart. As you take this position, be aware that you may need to devote more effort to staying awake!

Close your eyes and enjoy the experience of relaxing your physical body.

As your body relaxes, so will your mind. Pay attention to your breath and imagine that each inhalation is filling your body with peace and harmony, while each exhalation expels all negativity. Breathe slowly and gently, counting each time you exhale. The breathing helps you relax, and the counting occupies your mind and prevents it from wandering. If you are new to meditation, you might decide to stop when you reach a predetermined target, such as twenty-five or thirty breaths, but you can continue for as long as you wish. You can gradually extend the number as you gain experience.

Be an observer and notice your thoughts as they come and go. Realize that they're only thoughts and allow them to pass through your mind. There's a possibility that a passing thought might trigger anger, stress, or some other emotion. If this happens, don't try to fight it—simply experience it and then let it go. The more you practice, the less frequently this will happen, and you will quickly notice when it does.

After five minutes or your predetermined number of exhalations, become aware of the outside world, and tell yourself that you'll return to full consciousness at the count of five. Count slowly up to five and open your eyes.

Drink a glass of water and think about your meditation experience for a few minutes before carrying on with your day.

Once you become used to meditating, you can experiment by focusing on an object about six feet in front of you. It can be anything you wish: a candle flame, a spot on the wall, a beautiful flower, or some other object. Gazing at an object will help you decide if you prefer meditating with your eyes open or closed.

If possible, set aside time for meditation every day. It will soon become a habit, and you'll find you'll be able to enter into a meditative state almost as soon as you get into a comfortable position.

Once meditation has become a regular part of your everyday life, you can take it to a new level by involving the angelic realms. You might meditate inside your magic circle after performing the Angelic Invocation of Protection in chapter 2. You can communicate with your guardian angel, ask different angels for advice, and pray while meditating.

With practice, you'll find you can meditate for longer periods of time. Instead of counting each exhalation, you might silently say to yourself "in" while inhaling and "out" as you exhale. Once you've reached a relaxed, meditative state, you might start repeating a word or short phrase to yourself, such as "peace," "truth," "happiness," and so on. You can meditate on different aspects of your life, such as your career, partner, family member, mortgage, or garden to gain amazing insights.

You can also develop spiritually by meditating on spiritual words or phrases, for example: faith, God, reincarnation, blessings, compassion, gratitude, guidance, interconnectedness, intuition, soul, spirit, transcendence, and universal love.

Contact specific angels by meditating on their name. If you don't know the name of a particular angel, meditate on the phrases "angel of abundance" (or whatever topic you would like to explore), or "guardian angel" if that is who you are wanting to contact.

Here's a special meditation to use when you want to contact a specific angel or the angelic realms.

Angel Meditation

Start by getting into a meditative state in your usual way.

When you feel relaxed, continue focusing on your breathing for at least sixty seconds.

Picture yourself in your mind's eye surrounded by an aura of many different colors. You realize that this is an extension of yourself and that the aura has expanded internally as well to revitalize every cell of your body. You notice that each time you exhale, your aura grows slightly larger until it has completely filled the room you're in with light, color, and divine energy.

Silently ask an angel or angels to come into your aura and make themselves known to you. If possible, ask for a specific angel.

The response can happen in a number of ways. You may suddenly have a sense of knowing that an angel is with you. You may feel the angel's energy or sense a slight breeze on your skin. You may "see" angels inside your aura or flashes of light.

Once you know that the angel is with you, ask if they have a message for you. You may not receive a reply the first few times you try this. If this happens, thank them for visiting you and say that you'll contact them again in a day or two. If you receive a response to your question, enjoy a silent conversation with the angel and say that you'd like to talk with them on a regular basis.

No matter what happens, thank them for visiting you and protecting and looking after you.

After saying goodbye, pay attention to your breathing again. Allow the visualization of your aura to gradually fade away. This meditation can be emotional, so it's a good idea to stay seated or lying down quietly for a few minutes before opening your eyes and getting up.

Once you are ready to start moving again, spend a few minutes thinking about the meditation you've just had. Don't forget to drink some water before carrying on with your day.

Walking with an Angel Meditation

Walking is a wonderful way to communicate with your guardian angel, or any other angel you wish to communicate with. Some people find it difficult to enter a meditative state while walking because their thoughts flow from one thing to another, sometimes influenced by what they experience as they walk but more often due to thinking about problems, worries, and other concerns while on the walk.

The easiest way to meditate while out walking is to start by focusing on your breathing using a technique nomadic people use to travel hundreds of kilometers a day over difficult and often hostile terrain.

In the early 1980s, Édouard G. Stiegler was on an economic mission for the United Nations in Kabul, Afghanistan, when he met a group of nomads who had just completed a 700-kilometer (435-mile) walk over deserts and mountains in just twelve days. He observed them and discovered the secret to their endurance was the connection between their breathing and their steps. When he returned to Paris, he wrote a book called *Regeneration Through the Afghan March* (originally published in 1981 as *Régénération par la marche afghane*).

The technique involves breathing in while taking three steps, holding the breath on the fourth step, exhaling on the next three steps, holding the breath for one step, and then starting the cycle over again.

The only rule of Afghan walking is to breathe through your nose because the nasal cavities produce nitric oxide, which greatly increases the amount of oxygen in the blood.[2] There are many health benefits associated with using the Nomad or Afghan walking method, including improving endurance, stimulating blood circulation and basal metabolic function, strengthening the immune system, slowing down the aging process, and decreasing stress.[3] For our purposes, another benefit of the Afghan walk is that it enables us to quickly and easily enter into a desired meditative state.

Exercise: Afghan Walking Meditation

Start by walking in your usual manner. After a minute or two, align your steps with your breathing and do the Afghan walk: Breathing through your nose, inhale while taking three steps, hold the breath on the fourth step, exhale on the next three steps, hold that for one

---

2. Annabel Streets, *52 Ways to Walk* (London: Bloomsbury Publishing, 2022), 24.

3. Oliver Adey, "The Afghan walk, the benefits of a regenerating walk," Get to Text website, October 9, 2020, https://gettotext.com/the-afghan-walk-the-benefits-of-a-regenerating-walk/.

step, then repeat. You might have to concentrate on your walking and breathing for a few minutes until it becomes automatic.

Once you've reached a relaxed and meditative state, start talking with your guardian angel. If your guardian angel is whom you want to talk to, continue the conversation for as long as you wish. If you want to talk to another angel for a specific purpose, ask your guardian angel to invite that angel to join you.

The specialist angel will arrive in a matter of seconds, and you can start talking and asking questions right away. I usually converse silently, but you can speak out loud if you wish. The answers will come as thoughts in your mind.

When you've gained the answers you need, thank the angel and say goodbye. You can continue talking with your guardian angel for as long as you wish. Your guardian angel is always with you, so you don't need to say goodbye. However, do make sure to take the opportunity to express your thanks for everything your guardian angel does for you.

To gain the full health benefits of the Afghan walk, try to walk for at least thirty minutes, even if you're not meditating for that length of time.

In practice, you might have to go into and out of the Afghan walk at times. If you're pausing to cross a road, for instance, you'll need to pay close attention to what you're doing and may have to walk briskly or even run to get to the other side. On my walks, I sometimes stop to talk with someone I encounter, which takes me out of my rhythm. My daily walk includes a section that has a steep incline, and I don't worry about my rhythm until the path levels out again. Don't worry about small interruptions; you'll be able to return to the meditation as soon as you resume the Afghan walk again.

Crystals

Crystals and gems have been considered valuable for thousands of years and were probably the first precious objects ancient humans owned and cherished. Throughout history, people have believed that these beautiful crystals and stones possess magical properties.

You can use any crystal or gemstone you wish to communicate with angels. The only rule is that it must appeal to you. On many occasions, I've gone into a crystal store to buy a particular gemstone but left with a different stone that happened to "speak" to me.

The following list has several stones; hopefully one or more will "speak" to you:

Amethyst: A violet stone often worn to provide peace of mind, reduce stress, and gain protection. It enhances psychic awareness, and is useful for meditation, channeling, and angelic communication.

Angelite: This beautiful blue stone is said to dispel negativity and enhance compassion, love, inner peace, and forgiveness. People frequently hold angelite while meditating and communicating with angels, especially their guardian angel.

Celestite (also known as celestine): This stone varies in color, ranging from white to red. It is usually found in a beautiful delicate sky-blue color, hence its name, derived from the Latin *coelestis*, which means "heavenly." It is used to create a strong and powerful connection with the spiritual realms.

Kunzite: A beautiful pink stone that balances the heart chakra, and creates loving, harmonious relationships.

Green prehnite: This stone is often used for healing and enhancing creativity. It is also used for communicating with the angelic realms, especially Archangel Raphael.

Rose quartz: Partly due to its color and largely because of its loving vibrations, this stone is known as the love stone; it helps people attract love of all kinds.

Selenite: Named after Selene, Greek goddess of the moon. It's a soft, colorless-to-clear white stone that relates to honesty, truth, and mental clarity. Because of its association with the moon, selenite is often associated with love, fertility, intuition, and the subconscious. It is frequently used to attract angels.

How to Look After Your Crystals and Gemstones

Crystals need to be looked after and treated with love, as they absorb both negative and positive energies from their environment. In addition to cleansing them regularly, it's a good idea to cleanse your crystals as soon as possible after purchasing them to eliminate any negativity they may have picked up before coming into your possession. You should also cleanse your crystals before and after use, as well as whenever you feel they have become dull or lacking in energy and need a boost of positivity.

The most important part of a cleansing is your intention. There are many ways to perform a cleansing, but no matter what method you choose, hold the intention that the cleansing will remove all the negativity surrounding the stone.

The simplest way to cleanse a crystal is to hold it in your cupped hands and blow onto it while thinking of your intent. Turn the crystal around between each exhalation to make sure that every part of the crystal receives your breath.

Another easy way to cleanse your crystal is to bury it overnight in a bowl of raw brown rice. White rice works well too, but I prefer to use brown. In the morning, wipe your crystal with a soft cloth and dispose of the rice. Don't eat it, as it will have absorbed all the negativity from your crystal.

Hold the crystal in your cupped hands and say a simple prayer to the Universal Life Force. You might say something along the lines of: "Infinite Spirit (or whatever name you choose for the Divine), please clear all the negative energies inside this crystal, so that it can be used for the good of everyone. Thank you. Amen." A friend of mine says the Lord's Prayer while holding his crystal. Again, what's important is the intent—you can cleanse a crystal by holding it while saying a mantra or a traditional prayer, if you wish.

Fill a drinking glass with dried sage and bury your crystal in it for twenty-four hours. The sage neutralizes all the negative energy in the crystal and replaces it with positivity. After you've done this, dispose of the sage by burning or burying it. You can also use dried rose petals, frankincense, myrrh, sandalwood, or any combination of dried herbs.

There are many other ways to cleanse crystals and gemstones, but the ones covered here are all safe and easy to do.

After cleansing your crystal, place it in direct sunlight for five or six hours to energize it.

How to Dedicate Your Crystal

The final step before using your crystal is to dedicate it to whatever purpose you have in mind. Here are two ways to do this.

Method One

Start by creating a short phrase or sentence that describes what you want your crystal to do. As this is an intention, I usually start the phrase with the words "I intend this crystal ..." followed by whatever it is I want the crystal to do. For instance, I might decide on, "I intend this crystal to help me contact the angelic realms." If I was wanting to contact a specific angel, I could say, "I intend this crystal to help me contact (angel's name)."

Once you've decided on a suitable intention, sit and relax with your crystal resting between the palms of your hands. Repeat your intention several times silently or out loud. I prefer to say my intentions out loud, but this is not always possible.

You can start using your crystal as soon as you've dedicated your crystal once, but you'll achieve better results if you repeat the dedication every day for at least seven days. This repetition ensures that your crystal is properly programmed.

Method Two

Sit down comfortably and take a few slow, deep breaths. Place your crystal in your left palm and rest the back of this hand in your right palm.

Start talking to your crystal. Either silently or out loud, let your crystal know why you want to communicate with angels. Also tell your crystal about your life and your hopes and dreams.

When you've shared all you want to, tell your crystal that you're going to fill it to overflowing with positive energy to ensure that you have a permanent connection with the angelic realms.

Visualize a clear white light entering the top of your head and flowing through your body to your left palm. In your mind's eye, "see" it filling the crystal with pure light. Continue focusing on the crystal until it's completely filled with white light and you see it totally surrounded by this pure light.

Sit silently and wait for a response. You might experience a sensation in your left palm as the crystal responds. You might hear music or words inside your head. You may feel an overwhelming sensation of peace and love. It makes no difference what response you receive—no matter how it comes, it's a message from the angels.

Sit quietly for a few minutes, thank your crystal, and then get up to continue with your day.

How to Keep Your Crystal

Whenever possible, keep your crystal somewhere where it will receive sunlight and fresh air. Crystals like natural surfaces, so place them on wood, glass, silk, and other natural fibers. It's fine to transport your crystals in closed boxes, but don't store them in a closed environment.

How to Work with Your Crystal

Once your crystal is dedicated, you'll find it increasingly useful whenever you wish to contact the angelic realms. The more you use it, the more receptive it will become, and you'll quickly find that you can communicate almost as soon as you pick it up.

Hold your crystal or keep it nearby whenever you're communicating, and keep it on your altar or in a safe place when you're not using it.

Now that you know a number of ways to communicate with angels, read on to learn how to contact a specific angel in the next chapter.

Chapter Three

How to Contact
a Particular Angel

You can contact any angel you wish. Some people hesitate to contact the best-known archangels—Raphael, Michael, Gabriel, and Uriel—thinking they're too busy to help, but this isn't the case. Every angel is more than willing to help you whenever you need it. There's no need to hesitate, delay, or hold back. If you haven't contacted angels before, you'll probably find that the best way to start is to establish and maintain regular contact with your guardian angel.

Your Guardian Angel

Everyone has a guardian angel. These special angels provide guidance, protection, and companionship from the moment their charges are born until the moment they die.

The concept of guardian angels began thousands of years ago in Mesopotamia in the Middle East, where people believed everyone had a personal god called *massar sulmi*, "guardian of people's safety."

Guardian angels are also mentioned several times in the Bible. In Matthew 18:10, when Jesus was talking about children, he said: "Take heed that ye despise not one of these little ones; for I say unto you, That in heaven their angels do always behold the face of my Father which is in heaven."

Your guardian angel's sole task is to guide and look after you throughout your life. It's highly likely that your guardian angel also looked after you in previous lifetimes and will continue to look after you in your future lives. Your guardian angel should therefore be the first angel to contact whenever you need angelic help or advice.

Sometimes, you may wish to contact other angels. If you need help urgently, for instance, call on Archangel Michael. If you want to deal with a problem in a diplomatic way, Yeiayel would be a good choice. There are angels for almost every purpose you could think of, and they're all at your disposal when you need them. The appendix contains a list of the most common concerns people have as well as the angels you can call on to overcome them.

Writing a Letter

Writing a letter to a specific angel is one of the best ways to make contact because writing forces you to think about how you want to word your need or concern. In addition, the concentration involved in sitting down and writing a letter often means that you and the angel will start communicating with each other before you've finished writing the letter.

Write to the angel in the same way you'd write to a good friend; a friendly, chatty letter works better than a formal, business-like one. Tell the angel what's going on in your life. Start by writing about your family and your hopes and dreams. Only after you've done that, ask the angel for whatever it is you need.

Most of the time, you'll be writing for a specific purpose and will need to describe what you want in as much detail as possible. The act of writing everything down puts your problems and concerns in perspective and helps you gain a clearer idea of the particular outcome you want. Remember that the angels have a much broader view of the situation than you. Although you might want a specific outcome, the angels might see something that will be better for you in the near future rather than immediately. For this reason it's better to ask for something that will be in your highest good and works well for everyone involved.

Can you still write to an angel even if you don't have a specific problem? Certainly! You can write a letter to any angel or angels you wish to ask for a closer connection or thank for a positive outcome.

Before finishing the letter, thank the angel for reading and express your hope that your request will be granted. Finally, express your love and sign the letter. Seal the letter in an envelope and write the name of the angel you've written to on the front.

Sending a Letter

Next, send the letter to your specific angel. Here are two ways to do it. Note that the first method involves lighting a candle. There are always risks when working with fire. I place my candles on metal trays and have a container of water nearby, in case of accidents and suggest you do the same. I have never had any problems but know people who have. Always be cautious when working with fire.

Light a candle, sit about six feet away from it, and gaze at the flame. Rest the back of your right hand on your left palm and place your left thumb on your right palm. (If you're left-handed, you might prefer to place the back of your left hand on your right palm.) The letter should rest on your right palm and be held in place with your left thumb.

While gazing at the candle flame, think about the angel to whom you've written the letter. If it's your guardian angel, think about all the things this special angel does for you. If you're contacting an angel for a special purpose, think about what you know about this angel and your reasons for making contact. Don't rush this stage. If you sit quietly, you may feel the angel's presence. If this happens, you'll be able to have a silent communication with them. However, it's more likely that you'll feel a sense of love and protection surrounding you like an invisible embrace.

When the time seems right, burn the envelope in the candle flame and watch the smoke rise upward to your angel. Say a silent thank-you when the envelope and letter have been completely consumed, and stand up feeling confident that the particular angel has received your message.

You might prefer to "post" your letter rather than burn it. The angels receive the letter as you write it, so perhaps you'd like to keep it. One good way to do this is to place the letter in its sealed envelope under your pillow. Keep it there for seven nights or until the letter is answered.

A good friend of mine has two boxes on her altar. The first box is her worries and concerns box. Whenever she has a problem, she writes whatever it is on a piece of paper and places it in this box. When she talks with her angels, she asks them to help her deal with the problems placed in that box. Every few weeks, she reads the slips of paper and disposes of the ones that have been resolved. She calls the other her angel mailbox. She places all the letters she writes to different angels in this box. At least once a week, she'll read the letters in the box and remove the ones that have been answered. My friend reports that as a result of doing this, her life has become easier and happier. She no longer worries about the difficulties and problems in her life, as she knows the angels will take care of them. She finds writing letters to angels therapeutic, and her practice has enabled her to gain an increasingly close relationship with the angelic realms.

Angels of the Elements

The concept of the four elements—air, fire, water, and earth—has roots in ancient Greek philosophy and has been adopted by many cultures and belief systems throughout history.

The four elements are often used symbolically to represent different aspects of human experience. They make a useful framework for exploring and understanding the different forces and qualities that shape our lives.

People work with the four elements for a variety of reasons, but here are a few of the most common:

Symbolism and representation: The four elements can be used to represent different aspects of the natural world, our personalities, and spiritual or magical concepts. For example, earth might represent someone who is stable and grounded, while air might represent intellectualism and communication.

Energy manipulation: Each element has its own unique energy that people work with to achieve specific outcomes. For example, you might work with the Archangel Michael (element of fire) to boost your confidence or passion, or work with Archangel Gabriel (element of water) to enhance your intuition or emotional sensitivity.

Ritual and ceremony: The four elements are often incorporated into rituals and ceremonies. A magical ritual might involve calling upon the four great archangels (Raphael, Michael, Gabriel, and Uriel) to create a sacred circle, with each element representing a different direction. The Angelic Invocation of Protection in chapter 2 is an example of this.

Personal growth and exploration: You might like to work with the angels of the different elements to gain self-understanding and explore your relationship with the natural world. By exploring the different energies and qualities associated with the angels of each element, you'll gain insights into your own strengths and weaknesses and develop a deeper sense of connection to the world around you.

Communicating with angels: Working with the four elements is a practical way to contact angels who can help you with your specific needs. You could, for instance, work with the angels of water if you wanted to attract a romantic relationship, or the angels of air if you wanted to express yourself more effectively.

Here are some of the correspondences for each element.

Air

Air is associated with the intellect, communication, and freedom. It is often linked to the qualities of clarity, objectivity, and innovation. It represents the realm of thought and the power of the mind.

Direction: East

Color: Yellow

Archangel: Raphael

Jewel: Topaz or chalcedony

Angel: Chassan

Metal: Mercury

Age: Birth

Season: Spring

Astrological signs: Gemini, Libra, and Aquarius

Tarot suit: Swords

The angels of air will help you in any matters involving clarity, discernment, discrimination, contentment, logic, understanding, learning, knowledge, inspiration, happiness, career, finances, communication, technology, travel, and truth. They can also be called upon for help in tests and examinations. The angels of air help you control negative feelings and emotions such as anxiety, fear, insecurity, lack of confidence, and impulsiveness.

Fire

The element of fire is often associated with energy, passion, and transformation. It is linked to the qualities of creativity, courage, and ambition. It represents the power of change, growth, and the ability to overcome obstacles.

Direction: South

Color: Red

Archangel: Michael

Jewel: Fire opal

Angel: Aral

Metal: Iron or gold

Age: Youth

Season: Summer

Astrological signs: Aries, Leo, and Sagittarius

Tarot suit: Wands

The angels of fire are willing to help you in any matters involving change, energy, enthusiasm, bravery, independence, inspiration, abundance, ambition, courage, drive, authority, leadership, motivation, power, purification, and strength. They can also help you control negative feelings, such as anger, hate, covetousness, jealousy, lust, possessiveness, vanity, violence, selfishness, and egotism.

Water

Water represents emotion, intuition, and adaptability. It is linked to the qualities of empathy, sensitivity, and flexibility. It represents the fluidity of life and the power of transformation through receptivity.

Direction: West

Color: Blue

Archangel: Gabriel

Jewel: Aquamarine or beryl

Angel: Taliahad

Metal: Silver

Age: Middle age

Season: Fall (Autumn)

Astrological signs: Cancer, Scorpio, and Pisces

Tarot suit: Cups

The angels of water will help you in any matters involving beauty, empathy, compassion, understanding, dreams, intuition, femininity, harmony, sensuality, sexuality, sympathy, understanding, and the subconscious. They can also help you deal with negative emotions, such as possessiveness, jealousy, deception, hatred, deceitfulness, backstabbing, treachery, and spite.

Earth

The element of earth represents stability, grounding, and materiality. It is associated with the physical realm and the material world. It is often linked to the qualities of patience, endurance, and practicality.

Direction: North

Color: Black

Archangel: Uriel

Jewel: Quartz

Angel: Phorlach

Metal: Lead

Age: Old age

Season: Winter

Astrological signs: Taurus, Virgo, and Capricorn

Tarot suit: Pentacles

Health and the Elemental Angels

The elemental angels are willing to discuss health matters with you. Chassan, the angel of air, will provide help with concerns about breathing. Aral, the angel of fire, will help with energy, circulation, respiration, and digestion. Taliahad, the angel of water, will help with concerns about blood and bodily fluids. Phorlach, the angel of earth, will provide help for any matters involving bones, muscles, and skin.

How to Contact the Angels of the Elements

You can contact the angels of the elements using any of the methods in chapter 2. You can also create a ritual designed specifically for them.

The first step is to collect some items to represent the four elements. If you don't have objects to symbolize the four elements, you can use a candle to symbolize all four of them: the candle and wick represent the element of earth, the dripping wax symbolizes water, the flame is fire, and the flickering symbolizes air. Now you know why people make a wish before blowing out the candles on their birthday cakes—the wish is actually their intention. Knowingly or not, these people are all performing magic. Although a candle is all that you need, it's a good idea to collect some attractive items to represent each of the elements whenever possible.

A ceremonial dagger is traditionally used to represent the element of air, but any sharp knife will work well. If you prefer, you can use a wind instrument, such as a flute or recorder.

Wands symbolize authority, power, and magic, as well as the element of fire. You can buy specially made wands in New Age stores and online, but an attractive branch between one and two feet in length works just as well. If possible, try to find a branch that has already fallen from a tree.

Traditionally, a chalice is used to symbolize the element of water. A wine glass will work just as well. Alternatively, you can use any attractive object that is capable of holding water.

Traditionally, a circular disc called a pentacle was used to symbolize the element of earth. A pentagram is inscribed on the front and a hexagram on the back. The pentagram symbolized the microcosm (humankind) and the hexagram the macrocosm (the universe). A round wooden platter works just as well and is arguably more useful, as it can hold fruit or cake. Other possibilities are a drum or an earthenware container of rock salt.

Consecration

Before using your four elemental objects to communicate with angels, they will need to be consecrated. This is a simple ritual that you can perform in front of your altar. In addition to the four items, place some salt, a candle, and a small container of water on your altar.

Before starting, have a bath or shower, and change into clean, loose-fitting clothes.

Stand in front of your altar and light the candle.

Visualize yourself and your altar surrounded by a circle of protection. If you prefer, you might like to construct the Angelic Invocation of Protection in chapter 2.

Face east and ask Chassan, the angel of air, for a blessing. Pause until you sense that the blessing has been given. Turn to face south and ask Aral, the angel of fire, for a blessing. Again, wait until you feel you have received it, and then turn to face west, and ask Taliahad, the angel of water, for a blessing. After you've received it, face north and ask Phorlakh for a blessing. Turn to face east again. You are now protected and safe inside your circle and can start consecrating the special objects you have collected.

Stand in front of your altar and pick up the object you decided will symbolize air. Let's assume that it's a dagger. Hold the dagger high in the air for a few seconds before bringing it down and passing it through the smoke produced by the candle. While you're doing this, say: "I hereby purify and consecrate you with the strength and power provided by the element of air."

Hold the dagger up high for a few moments and then pass it through the flame of the candle while saying: "I hereby purify and consecrate you with the strength and power provided by the element of fire." Visualize a powerful flame removing all the negativity from the dagger.

Hold the dagger up high again, and then place it gently on the altar. Dip your fingers into the container of water and sprinkle the dagger with a few drops of water while saying: "I hereby purify and consecrate you with the strength and power created by the element of water." Visualize a stream of purifying water washing away any negativity that remains attached to the dagger.

Pick up the dagger and hold it high again for a few moments. Place it back on your altar and sprinkle it with a few grains of salt while saying: "I hereby purify and consecrate you with the strength and power provided by the element of earth." Visualize the dagger buried in earth and being drained of all negativity.

Repeat this process with the other three objects. Once you've done that, place the four objects in a row at the front of your altar and thank them for becoming your sacred objects.

When you feel ready, close the ritual by thanking the angels of the elements in turn. Start by facing Chassan in the east. Say thank you, smile, and wave goodbye. Turn to face Phorlakh in the north and again smile and wave goodbye as you express your thanks. Repeat this with Taliahad in the west and Aral in the south. Finish by facing east again, and spend a minute or two in quiet contemplation before snuffing out the candle and leaving the circle.

You will have noticed that you asked the angels for a blessing in a clockwise order. When you thanked them and said goodbye, you started with the same angel (Chassan) but then moved in a counter-clockwise direction.

Your special objects have now been consecrated and are ready for use. You need to treat them with respect. Don't let anyone else handle them, and store them safely when you're not using them. You might like to wrap them in silk to keep them safe before putting them away.

Elemental Angel Ritual

Here is a basic ritual that you can use as a template for any elemental angel ritual that you create for your needs.

Before starting, place a white candle and your elemental sacred objects on your altar. Enjoy a leisurely bath and change into clean, loose-fitting clothes. If you don't have a bath, a shower works almost as well. The advantage of a bath is that you can relax in the warm water and think about the ritual you're about to perform. After the bath, you might like to put on a robe or some other garment that you wear only when performing rituals.

This ritual is conducted inside a magic circle. You can create a circle approximately eight to twelve feet in diameter by placing small objects such as gemstones, river stones, or ornaments in a circle to indicate the circumference. You might prefer to use a length of rope to mark out the circle. Alternatively, instead of a physical circle, you can visualize a circle of whatever size you wish.

Stand in front of your altar and light the candle.

Close your eyes, and in your mind's eye see yourself and your altar inside your magic circle. Visualize a pure white light descending from the heavens and filling your circle with divine love and protection.

Pick up your dagger in your right hand and face east. Point the dagger slightly upward in front of you and call on Chassan, the angel of air, silently or out loud, using whatever words you wish. You might call out: "Hello Chassan, angel of air. I'm conducting a ritual and need your help. Please join me." Wait until you sense that Chassan is with you, and then replace the dagger on your altar.

Pick up the wand in your right hand and face south. Hold your wand up high and ask Aral, the angel of fire, to join you. When you receive a response, place the wand back on your altar.

Pick up the chalice and face west. Hold it in both hands at approximately shoulder height. Ask Taliahad, angel of water, to join you. When you sense Taliahad's presence, replace the chalice on your altar.

Pick up the pentacle and face north. If you have a traditional pentacle, hold it up high in your right hand. If you're using a wooden dish or bowl, hold it at chest height with both hands. Ask Phorlakh to join you. When you receive a response, place the object back on the altar.

You are now protected and safe inside your magic circle. Spend a minute or two enjoying the pleasant sensations of warmth and security. As you turn around, enjoy feeling the energies of the four angels of the elements.

When you feel totally relaxed and comfortable inside your circle, turn to face the angel who relates best to whatever your need happens to be and make your request. Engage the angel in conversation, making sure to include the other three angels guarding your circle in the discussion. Pause every now and again to give them plenty of time to respond to what you are saying. Speak in a normal, conversational manner, as if you were talking to close friends—which, as it happens, is exactly what you are doing. Take as long as you wish. The angels are there to help you and will not grow impatient if you take your time. Sometimes the conversation might be over in a matter of minutes, while at others it could take an hour or more. The angels won't mind, and want you to mention everything you'd like to discuss.

When you have finished your conversation, it's time to thank the angels for their help, support, and love. Thank them jointly, and again separately, as you say goodbye. Ask them to send your request to the Divine. Say goodbye first to Chassan, angel of the east, and then work counterclockwise until you finish with Aral in the south.

Face east and pause for a minute or two before snuffing out the candle, and leaving the circle.

Leave your sacred objects on the altar until you've finished changing back into your normal clothes. You'll find that your consecrated objects will gain more spiritual energy every time you use them.

Make sure to ground yourself after the ritual by having something to eat and drink. When I perform this ritual on my own, I usually eat a handful of nuts and raisins and drink a glass of water. If I'm performing it with friends, I'll eat cookies and cake and enjoy a glass of wine.

Angels of the Zodiac

As angels, stars, and planets are all connected with the celestial realms, it's not surprising that angels have been associated with the signs of the zodiac for thousands of years. According to Jewish tradition, Masleh is the angel in charge of the zodiac and the medium through which the Divine transmits power and influence to each sign of the zodiac.

You can call on the angels of the zodiac to help you in any matters relating to the qualities of a specific sign. These angels are effectively the guardian angels that look after each sign. You can call on the angel ruling your horoscope sign whenever you wish, which is especially useful when you want information that relates to your future. When making a request for someone else, use the angel who looks after their sign. You can also call on any of the zodiacal angels whenever you need some of the qualities associated with the sign.

Aries: Machidiel

Color: Red

Planet: Mars

Element: Fire

Machidiel (sometimes known as Malahidael) is the angel of March and is responsible for everyone born under the sign of Aries. You can call on Machidiel whenever you need to gain strength to stand up for what you believe is true and right. Machidiel also helps people gain the necessary courage to express their love to others. Machidiel gives people hope and helps them start again after setbacks and disappointments.

Taurus: Asmodel

Color: Yellow, pink, pale blue

Planet: Venus

Element: Earth

Asmodel rules over the month of April and looks after people born under the sign of Taurus. Asmodel is one of the angels of patience and encourages slow but steady progress. He is frequently called upon to help people remain focused on their goals as well as to increase their net worth. He enjoys helping people on any matter involving love and romance. Asmodel also helps people create beauty in every aspect of their lives. According to legend, at one time Asmodel was one of the cherubim who guarded the entrance to the Garden of Eden. Unfortunately, he was demoted after the rebellion in heaven. However, he retained his love of nature and can be called upon by anyone who needs help with agriculture and gardening, or wants to increase their appreciation of nature.

Gemini: Ambriel

Color: Violet, yellow

Planet: Mercury

Element: Air

Ambriel governs the month of May and is responsible for everyone born under the sign of Gemini. Ambriel can be called upon for any matters involving communication and self-expression. Ambriel enjoys helping people who are looking for new opportunities and responsibilities. Artists often depict Ambriel with one hand raised to ward off evil, as he is known for his discernment between right and wrong.

Cancer: Muriel

Color: Green, gray, silver

Planet: Moon

Element: Water

Muriel governs to the month of June and looks after people born under the sign of Cancer. Muriel is the angel of peace and harmony. She has a special interest in helping people in close relationships. She also helps people who are sick or in pain. You can call on Muriel whenever you need help in controlling your emotions. Muriel also enjoys helping people develop their intuition.

Leo: Verchiel

Color: Orange, gold

Planet: Sun

Element: Fire

Verchiel governs the month of July and is responsible for people born under the sign of Leo. Verchiel provides enthusiasm, energy, and a positive, playful outlook on life. Verchiel encourages people to make the most of every moment and to let go of grievances from the past. She has a special interest in helping people who are seeking friendship, affection, and love. You can also call on Verchiel whenever you're having problems with family members or friends.

Virgo: Hamaliel

Color: Violet, navy blue, dark gray

Planet: Mercury

Element: Earth

Hamaliel governs the month of August and looks after everyone born under the sign of Virgo. Hamaliel is willing to help people with any matters that involve clear thinking, logic, and attention to detail. Hamaliel encourages cooperation with others and a practical approach to problem solving. She also encourages patience and recommends slow but steady progress toward achieving your goals.

Libra: Zuriel

Color: Yellow, pale blue, pink, green

Planet: Venus

Element: Air

Zuriel governs the month of September and is responsible for people born under the sign of Libra. Zuriel can be called upon to create harmony and improve relationships. He encourages people to be calm in difficult situations rather than overreact, and to compromise when necessary. Zuriel is also the angel of childbirth and is sometimes invoked to ease a mother's pain.

Scorpio: Barbiel

Color: Maroon, dark red

Planet: Pluto

Element: Water

Barbiel governs the month of October and is responsible for people born under the sign of Scorpio. You can call on Barbiel to heal physical and emotional pain, as well as to learn from past mistakes. Barbiel is also willing to help you develop your intuition and compassion. Barbiel enjoys working with people who have big goals and are firmly focused on achieving them. According to legend, Barbiel is extremely interested in astrology.

Sagittarius: Adnachiel

Color: Purple

Planet: Jupiter

Element: Fire

Adnachiel (sometimes known as Advachiel) governs the month of November and looks after everyone born under the sign of Sagittarius. Adnachiel is known as the angel of independence and seeks opportunities to help people with adventurous dispositions. He encourages curiosity and learning as a lifelong endeavor. You can call on Adnachiel whenever you're forced outside your comfort zone and need additional help.

Capricorn: Anael
Color: Blue, dark green
Planet: Saturn
Element: Earth

Anael (sometimes known as Hanael or Haniel) governs the month of December and looks after people born under the sign of Capricorn. Anael is considered to be an angel of joy, love, and harmony. Consequently, he is frequently called upon by people who need help with any situations involving love, home, and family. Anael helps people who need emotional healing and can assist with maintaining good, healthy, harmonious relationships with others.

Aquarius: Cambiel
Color: Indigo
Planet: Uranus
Element: Air

Cambiel governs the month of January and is responsible for people born under the sign of Aquarius. Cambiel has a strong interest in science and technology and enjoys helping people who are interested in anything new and progressive. Cambiel encourages people to recognize and take advantage of their uniqueness and original approach to life.

Pisces: Barchiel

Color: Indigo, sea blue

Planet: Neptune

Element: Water

Barchiel (sometimes known as Barakiel) governs the month of February and looks after people born under the sign of Pisces. Barchiel helps people gain a more positive approach to life. Barchiel is considered an angel of good luck; under the name Barakiel, he is popular with gamblers or anyone interested in games of chance.

Angels of the Week

There are seven angels responsible for the different days of the week. Magicians call on these angels on their respective days to help them perform their rituals and magic at the best possible time. Over the years, many angels have been suggested for each day. For instance, a famous thirteenth-century grimoire called *Liber Juratus*, or *The Sworn Book of Honorius*, listed forty-seven angels for Sunday, fifty-six for Monday, fifty-two for Tuesday, forty-five for Wednesday, thirty-seven for Thursday, forty-seven for Friday, and fifty for Saturday. Fortunately, common sense finally prevailed; today, most people work with the seven archangels listed in *The Magus* by Francis Barrett, published in 1801. In the Bible, these archangels are described as "seven lamps of fire burning before the throne, which are the seven Spirits of God" (Revelation 4:5), and "the seven angels which stood before God" (Revelation 8:2).

Monday: Gabriel

Monday is connected with the moon, making this a good day to focus on any matters involving the psychic world, spirituality, dreams, emotions, health, nurturing, and feminine interests.

Tuesday: Camael (Chamuel)

Tuesday is connected with Mars. This day is good for any activities involving energy, courage, power, confidence, persistence, motivation, sexuality, and passion. Samael often assists Archangel Camael when he needs help on Tuesdays.

Wednesday: Raphael

Wednesday is associated with Mercury, making this a good day for all matters involving communication, eloquence, mediation, adaptation, technology, reason, intellect, and personal interests. Archangel Michael often assists Archangel Raphael when he needs help on this day.

Thursday: Sachiel

Thursday is connected with Jupiter. This day is ideal for matters related to opportunities, abundance, expansion, excitement, joy, benevolence, kindness, justice, and optimism. Tzaphiel often helps Archangel Sachiel when she needs help on this day and also helps Cassiel on Saturdays.

Friday: Anael

Friday is associated with Venus, therefore making this a good day for any activities that involve romance, love, pleasure, imagination, harmony, and happiness. Archangel Haniel often assists Anael when he needs help on this day. Their relationship is so close that Anael is sometimes mistakenly assumed to be Haniel.

Saturday: Cassiel

Saturday is connected with Saturn, so this day is best for dealing with challenges, restrictions, discipline, focus, contemplation, determination, persistence, and morality. Archangel Tzaphiel often assists Cassiel on Saturdays, and also helps Archangel Sachiel on Thursdays.

Sunday: Michael

Sunday is associated with the sun. This makes it a good day to focus on success, achievement, happiness, and masculine interests. Archangel Raphael assists Archangel Michael when he needs help on this day.

Most people associate angels with spirituality and religion, which isn't surprising considering most of what we know about angels comes from the sacred writings of different religions. All angels are angels of spirituality. However, a number of angels have a special interest in helping people discover and develop the spiritual sides of their lives. We'll look at the more important angels of spirituality in the next chapter.

Chapter Four

The Angels of Spirituality

More and more people today consider themselves spiritual. They are seekers who are responding to a deep inner longing to experience more from life than they currently receive from the mundane, everyday world they're living in. Many haven't received what they seek from religion and say, "I'm spiritual but not religious."

These people are seeking meaning and purpose in life. Spirituality often begins with the realization that there must be something greater than ourselves that is in control, that there is more to life than what we experience on sensory and physical levels, and that every one of us is part of the Divine.

In actuality, everyone is spiritual—we express our spirituality in everything we think, say, and do. The spiritual part of our lives is just as important as the physical, mental, and social aspects. We can't claim to be fully alive until we look beyond the temporal and open ourselves up for spiritual nourishment. It's spiritual to forgive others and to be kind, generous, caring, and compassionate. It's spiritual to express ourselves creatively. It's spiritual to exercise, socialize, laugh, and stand in awe at the beauty of nature. It's spiritual to love others as well as ourselves. Unfortunately, much of the time we're not fully aware of our spiritual dimension and lead lives that fail to reflect the pure divine love we were born with.

People get in touch with their spirituality in different ways. Meditation, prayer, communing with nature, and yoga are good examples. And of course, many people find spiritual fulfillment in different religious traditions, such as Christianity, Judaism, and Buddhism.

Today, many people develop their spiritual side and search for a closer connection to the Divine in their own way. They start understanding that they are meant to be alive at this time to pursue a sacred task, one that angels are often involved in. As angels carry messages to and from the Divine, they play an important role in helping people develop their own personal spirituality. In this capacity, they are sometimes referred to as angelic counselors.

Angelic Counselors

Counselors are people who are trained to give guidance to people on personal and psychological issues. They help people who are experiencing anxiety, stress, depression, financial issues, marital difficulties, and emotional problems. A counselor's aim is to effect change and restore their clients' innate feelings of well-being.

Angels are willing to provide help and guidance on any of the problems that people experience as they go through life, so they can certainly be considered counselors too. In addition, you have a limitless number of angels to call on when you need help. The best choice is usually your guardian angel because they are dedicated to you and your spiritual growth. Alongside them are the angels for every purpose. If, for instance, you're trying to get pregnant, you might call a council of angels and ask Armisael, Cahetel, Gabriel, Lailah, and Zuriel to help you. If you're suffering from depression, Azrael, Bath Kol, Isda, Metatron, Raziel, Rehael, and Remiel would be delighted to hold a council meeting with you (see chapter 2 for more information on how to hold a council meeting with a group of angels).

Your guardian angel, as well as every other angel, is more than willing to help you grow spiritually. In addition, Balthiel, Elemiah, Haamiah, Jegudiel, Melchizedek, Micah, Pahaliah, and Sandalphon are all specialists on this topic. All you need do is ask for help.

Balthiel is the angel of forgiveness and is frequently called upon by people who know they should forgive someone for something done to them but find it hard to do.

Elemiah plays a major role in Jewish scriptures and is said to belong to the Schemhamphoras, a group of seventy-two angels who bear the various names of God. In the Kabbalah, Elemiah is one of the eight seraphim of the Tree of Life. Elemiah looks after travelers, especially those traveling over water. He is also regularly invoked by people seeking inner and spiritual growth.

Haamiah is, like Elemiah, a member of the Schemhamphoras. He is considered the main angel of integrity and also looks after people who are genuinely seeking spiritual knowledge. (More information on Haamiah appears in chapter 13.)

The name Jegudiel means "the Glory of God." Jegudiel actively helps those seeking a closer relationship with God. He provides opportunities for sincere seekers who are prepared to work hard to achieve significant spiritual goals.

Melchizedek is said to be one of the most powerful angels in heaven. Dionysius the Areopagite wrote that he was the angel most loved and favored by God. According to Jewish legend, Melchizedek delivered God's covenant to Abraham and prepared the way for the coming of Jesus. Another legend says that he spent a hundred years on earth four thousand years ago and started a school to teach people about God. He is still performing similar work in heaven today. He is vitally interested in helping genuine spiritual seekers.

Micah focuses on the spiritual growth of mankind and is keen to help anyone who is pursuing a spiritual path.

Pahaliah is a member of the Schemhamphoras and encourages people to be honest, upright, and fair in everything they do. His main task is to encourage people to welcome the Divine into their lives.

Sandalphon is an important angel who is said to be the head of the guardian angels. Sandalphon helps Metatron in weaving Jewish prayers into garlands that God can wear on his head. Although his focus is on Jewish prayers, Sandalphon is also happy to carry anyone's prayer to heaven.

How to Pray with Angels

A prayer is a spiritual communion with the Divine or, more simply, talking to God (Divine Spirit, Architect of the Universe, Heavenly Father/Mother, Mother Earth, or whatever term you prefer). There are a number of reasons why people pray. They pray to give thanks to the Divine. They pray when they need help. They pray when they've done something wrong and want to be forgiven. They pray when they want to improve some aspect of themselves, such as to become kinder or to be a better listener.

Prayers do not need to be written or spoken in a formal manner. Start by addressing the deity by name and then talk as if you're speaking to a close friend. Give thanks for the blessings in your life and ask for help when it's required. Pray for others who need help or guidance. Finish by expressing your thanks. Prayers do not need to be long. Often, one sentence can be enough. "Thank you for all the good things in my life," and "Please help Aunty Jean," are both examples of short prayers that express their purpose in just a few words.

Angels are servants of the Divine. When you pray, it is to the Divine rather than to the angels. However, you can involve and include angels in your prayers. You might, for instance, ask your guardian angel to deliver your prayer for you or ask a specific angel who has a strong interest in the subject of your prayer to deliver it for you.

The one angel you should always include in your prayers is your guardian angel, who is dedicated solely to you and with whom you share an unbreakable spiritual bond. Over the last two thousand years, many prayers have been written that people can use when communicating with their guardian angel, but the one here is considered the most famous one. Although no one knows for certain who wrote this prayer, it is thought to have been written by Reginald of Canterbury, an eleventh-century Benedictine monk. You can say it at any time.

> Angel of God, my guardian dear,
> to whom God's love commits me here,
> ever this day be at my side,
> to light and guard, to rule and guide.
> Amen.

Praying with Your Guardian Angel

Here's an example of how to pray with the active help of your guardian angel and any other angels who relate to your needs at the time. It takes only a few minutes and can be done anywhere.

Take a slow, deep breath in, hold it for a few seconds, and then exhale slowly. The purpose of this breath is to help you slow down and relax.

On the second inhalation, visualize a pure white light descending from above that surrounds you and fills you with divine energy. As you exhale, let go of all the negativity you've been harboring in your body.

Continue taking slow, deep breaths, and visualize yourself surrounded by loving angels who are providing you with a constant flow of positive energy. Ask your guardian angel and any other angels you wish to talk with (such as the four great archangels) to let you know they're with you. You might experience a gentle touch, a feeling of safety and warmth, or just a feeling of certainty that they're there. Even if you don't experience anything, know that they're with you and are ready to do everything they can to help you.

When you feel the time is right, silently talk with your angels. Tell them what you want and need right now. Ask questions and listen carefully for any answers. Thank them for all the help they've given you in the past, and ask them to continue surrounding you with love.

Once you've finished talking with the angels, ask them to stay with you while you pray to the Divine. This can be as short or as long as you need. It might be a simple thank-you, a request for yourself or others, a recitation of a familiar prayer such as the Lord's Prayer, or resting quietly in the presence of the Divine.

When the time feels right, express your gratitude, and finish by saying "amen," "so be it," "I agree," or any other words that confirm your faith that your prayers will be answered in time.

How to Send Blessings to Others

Sending blessings to others is easy to do and will improve your life as well as the lives of others in many ways. It will help you realize that we are all one, and will also strengthen your connection with the Divine. The more frequently you do it, the more your spirituality will grow, and your relationships with everyone in your life will become better than they already are.

All you need is five to ten minutes of uninterrupted time.

Sit down in a comfortable chair, close your eyes, and take a few slow, deep breaths to help you relax and enter into a quiet space.

Ask your guardian angel to help you. Think of someone you love, and silently send a blessing to him or her. Your guardian angel will also send a blessing to that person.

Once you've blessed one person, think of someone else and send a blessing to them too. You can continue doing this for as long as you wish. You might like to start with family members, followed by friends, work colleagues, and acquaintances. It's good to start with the people you love and care for, but it's also important to include people you don't get on with or may even dislike.

Next, send a blessing to yourself. You are as worthy of receiving a blessing as anyone else.

Finish by sending a blessing to everyone in the world.

Sit quietly for a minute or two before opening your eyes and continuing with your day.

It's important that you do this anonymously. There's no need to tell others about this particular spiritual practice, as they might think you're inflating your own sense of importance. While it's true you are doing this for your own benefit, you are primarily sending blessings to others. The main purpose is to develop a sense of loving-kindness to everyone.

The benefits of this practice will become more and more apparent over time. Sending blessings to people on a regular basis will bring you closer to them, and you'll find that relationships that had previously been difficult will improve. In many cases, the problems will mysteriously disappear and you'll find your interactions with these people will gradually become more harmonious and enjoyable.

You can also send blessings to people and animals you don't know but happen to encounter in the course of your everyday life. You can bless people wherever you happen to be. It could be a stranger you pass on the way to work. It could be the barista at a local coffee shop.

Imagine how you'd feel if you blessed someone who cut you off on the freeway. Any feelings of anger or frustration you might have experienced when something like this occurred in the past will be replaced by love and kindness.

In the next chapter we'll start working with the four great archangels, starting with the one who is said to be God's favorite—Archangel Michael.

Chapter Five

How to Work with Archangel Michael

Archangel Michael works tirelessly to achieve peace and harmony in the world. Christians, Jews, and Muslims all consider him to be the greatest angel of all. Michael provides people with strength, courage, integrity, protection, sympathy, patience, and ambition. He also encourages and looks after people who are seeking to develop spiritually. The early Christian theologian Origen (ca. 185–ca. 253 CE) considered Michael to be the angel of prayer.

Clearing Energy Blocks

It would be hard to find anyone who hasn't experienced energy blocks that hold them back and prevent them from achieving their goals. Sometimes these are temporary blocks that are easily overcome, but others can be held for an entire lifetime. Most commonly, energy blocks are created by negative thoughts and emotions such as anger, fear, anxiety, worry, and depression.

People often call on Archangel Michael to help eliminate these problems, as his strength, spiritual power, and protection can help remove any negative or harmful energy blocks or influences that may be affecting them. In the process, Archangel Michael can also help remove negative energies; cut cords of attachment to anything that is draining energy; and provide spiritual guidance, purification, and protection.

Some people also believe that Archangel Michael can help release fear, increase self-confidence, and promote spiritual growth and development. Therefore, using his name or image during energy clearing increases the effectiveness of the clearing process and provides a sense of comfort and security. Archangel Michael can help you eliminate the energy blocks that hold you back and prevent you from being all that you could be.

Inside our auras and located alongside the spinal column are seven energy centers known as chakras. The word *chakra* is Sanskrit for "wheel." In different spiritual traditions of India, chakras are often depicted as lotus flowers, each one with a different number of petals. The chakras are revolving circles of subtle energies that transform higher energies and turn them into a form that can the body can use. They play an important role in the individual's physical, mental, and emotional health. Even though the chakras are non-physical, they have a powerful effect on how we function physically.

The human body contains currents of both positive and negative energies that come directly from the breath. The right side of the body carries the positive energies, and the left side the negative. These energies influence the directions the chakras revolve in, and each chakra appears to revolve in the opposite direction to the chakras immediately above and below it.

Earth energies enter our bodies through our feet and flow upward through the seven chakras, until they leave at the top of our heads and connect with the loving light of the universe. Simultaneously, spiritual energies enter our bodies at the top of our heads and flow through each of the chakras, gradually slowing down as they do so until they leave the body and connect with the energies of the earth. This means that everyone living on this planet is connected with the higher spiritual planes as well as the physical world.

The seven main chakras act as powerful energy centers that stimulate the subtle and physical bodies that they're responsible for. Each chakra is related to a physical system and the organs associated with it, and there is a direct relationship between the state of each chakra and the health of the organs it is connected to. The chakras can be open, closed, blocked, and both in or out of balance. It's rare to find anyone who has every chakra open and in balance. Most people experience fluctuations in the state of their individual chakras caused by stress, tension, frustration, and worry. Any changes that restore a chakra to balance have an immediate effect upon the physical body.

The chakra groups are often represented as a square and a triangle. The four bottom chakras (the square) have a slower vibration than the top three chakras, and each one is related to the traditional elements of earth, water, fire, and air. Collectively, they are known as the quatern.

Root Chakra

Color: Red

Element: Earth

Function: Survival

Glands: Adrenals

Petals: Four

Sense: Smell

Desires: Physical contact

Challenge: To think before acting

Keyword: Physical

The root chakra, sometimes called the base chakra, is situated at the base of the spine in the area of the coccyx. It keeps us firmly grounded to the earth, and is concerned with self-preservation. It controls our fight-or-flight responses. It also provides vitality, energy, and stimulation. At an emotional level, it provides strength, courage, and persistence. The root chakra also looks after the solid parts of our bodies, such as teeth, bones, and nails. It is also related to the sense of smell.

When this chakra is understimulated, the person will feel nervous and insecure, possibly leading to digestive problems along with fears, doubts, and confidence issues. When the root chakra is overstimulated, the person will be self-centered, domineering, and addicted to money, power, and sex.

Sacral Chakra

Color: Orange

Element: Water

Function: Sexuality, creativity, pleasure

Glands: Ovaries, testicles

Petals: Six

Sense: Taste

Desires: Respect and acceptance

Challenge: To love and serve others

Keyword: Social

The sacral chakra is situated in the lower abdomen, approximately two inches below the navel. Because this chakra is associated with the element of water, it's concerned with the fluidic functions of the body. It represents creativity, emotional balance, and sexuality. At an emotional level, it stimulates hope and optimism. It also relates to the sense of taste.

People with well-balanced sacral chakras relate well with others, having the necessary fluidity to interact and harmonize easily. If this chakra is blocked or out of balance, the person is likely to suffer from arthritis, urinary problems, sexual dysfunction, and a loss of personal power. These problems are often caused by the anger, frustration, and resentment that fester when this chakra is understimulated. If the sacral chakra is overstimulated, the person will be aggressive, manipulative, and excessively self-indulgent.

Solar Plexus Chakra

Color: Yellow

Element: Fire

Function: Will, personal power

Glands: Pancreas

Petals: Ten

Sense: Sight

Desires: To understand

Challenge: To communicate effectively with loved ones

Keyword: Intellect

The solar plexus chakra is situated between the navel and the breastbone (sternum). It gives us personal power, warmth, confidence, good self-esteem, and happiness. When it's working well, food is easily digested, absorbed, and assimilated, and the person experiences feelings of physical well-being. This chakra is also related to the eyes. The solar plexus chakra enhances creativity, optimism, confidence, trust, and self-respect. Anger and hostility can build up in this chakra when the person has a negative outlook on life. If this chakra is overstimulated, the person will become an overly demanding perfectionist and a workaholic. Conversely, if this chakra is understimulated, the person will lack confidence, be overly sensitive, and feel as if they have little or no control of their life. This feeling can cause ulcers and stomach disorders.

Heart Chakra

Color: Green

Element: Air

Function: Love

Glands: Thymus

Petals: Twelve

Sense: Touch

Desires: To love and be loved

Challenge: To gain confidence

Keyword: Emotions

The heart chakra is in the middle of the chest, in line with the heart. It relates to personal and unconditional love, harmony, sympathetic understanding, healing, and the sense of touch. At an emotional level, the heart chakra enhances compassion, self-acceptance, and respect for self and others. People with well-balanced heart chakras are in touch with their feelings. They nurture themselves and encourage and support others. When the heart chakra is understimulated, the person will be overly sensitive and sympathetic, and will feel sorry for themselves. Not surprisingly, most codependent people have an understimulated heart chakra. If the heart chakra is overstimulated, the person will be possessive, demanding, controlling, and moody.

The Trinity

The three uppermost chakras are symbolized by the triangle, and are collectively known as the trinity. They vibrate at a higher level than the four chakras of the quatern. This doesn't mean they are more important, as each chakra is essential, and they all work in together.

The three chakras of the trinity (the triangle) relate to the quadruplicities of astrology: cardinal, fixed, and mutable. The cardinal signs (Aries, Cancer, Libra, and Capricorn) are outgoing, expressive, energetic, and enjoy starting things. The fixed signs (Taurus, Leo, Scorpio, and Aquarius) are rigid, stubborn, tenacious, stable, and dependable. The mutable signs (Gemini, Virgo, Sagittarius, and Pisces) are adaptable and quick to adjust to changing circumstances.

Throat Chakra

Color: Blue

Quadruplicity: Fixed

Function: Communication, creativity

Glands: Thyroid and parathyroid

Petals: Sixteen

Sense: Sound

Desires: Inner peace

Challenge: To risk

Keyword: Concepts

The throat chakra is situated at the level of the throat. It is the chakra of communication and self-expression. It seeks the truth in all things. At an emotional level, the throat chakra enhances idealism, love, and understanding. When it is balanced, this chakra provides contentment, peace of mind, and a strong sense of faith. Someone with a balanced throat chakra will be kind and considerate when dealing with others. When the throat chakra is overstimulated, the person will be arrogant, domineering, overbearing, and sarcastic. They will speak constantly but will have little interest in listening to others. When this chakra is understimulated, the person will be weak, fearful, unreliable, and uncommunicative. They may experience neck and shoulder problems.

Brow Chakra

Color: Indigo

Quadruplicity: Mutable

Function: Intuition, thought, perception

Glands: Pituitary

Petals: Ninety-six

Desires: To be in harmony with the universe

Challenge: To turn one's dreams into reality

Keyword: Intuition

The brow chakra is situated in the center of the forehead just above the eyebrows. At an emotional level, this chakra helps us become aware of our spiritual natures. It enables us to pick up other people's thoughts, feelings, and intuitions. The brow chakra is often called the third eye, as it is concerned with spiritual and psychic matters. When this chakra is overstimulated, the person will be proud, authoritative, dogmatic, and have a strong sense of self-importance. When it is understimulated, the person will be timid, hesitant, and non-assertive. The person will experience stress and tension headaches.

Crown Chakra

Color: Violet

Quadruplicity: Cardinal

Function: Union with the Divine

Glands: Pineal

Petals: Nine hundred and seventy-two

Desires: Universal understanding

Challenge: To grow in knowledge and wisdom

Keyword: Spirituality

The crown chakra is situated at the top of the head. It harmonizes and balances the often-conflicting sides of our natures. It also governs the mystical and spiritual sides of our being to gain insight and understanding about the interconnectedness of all living things. It cannot be activated until all the other chakras are balanced. When the crown chakra is balanced, the person experiences enlightenment and has a sense of being at one with the entire universe. When this chakra is overstimulated, the person will feel frustrated, irritable, miserable, and destructive. Often, overstimulation leads to severe migraine headaches. When this chakra is understimulated, the person will be withdrawn, reticent, inhibited, and unable to recognize or experience any of the joys of life.

Archangels and the Chakras

In recent decades, many people have assigned angels and archangels to the seven chakras. Given that there were traditionally seven archangels and seven main chakras, it's a perfect fit. Most sources associate Raphael with the heart chakra and Michael with the throat chakra, but there's no agreement about any of the others. Association doesn't matter for our purposes; we can call on whichever angel we choose to release blockages and balance and harmonize our chakras.

When it all comes down to it, everyone wants to lead a happy, productive life surrounded by a loving family and good friends, working in a career they find fulfilling and enjoyable, and with a faith in themselves and in something greater that sustains them during difficult times. The fortunate people who achieve this manage to keep all seven of their main chakras balanced most of the time. They do this by:

- Looking after their physical bodies, keeping their feet on the ground, and working hard in the material world. These are all qualities of the root chakra.

- Enjoying pleasurable activities and focusing on positive rather than negative emotions. These are all provided by the sacral chakra.

- Being ambitious and achieving worthwhile goals. Seeking a degree of power and responsibility, and then using it wisely. These are qualities of the solar plexus chakra.

- Having a loving nature, and nurturing their hearts with both fulfilling personal relationships and universal love for all humanity. These are provided by the heart chakra.

- Thinking before acting, using their communication skills effectively, and making good use of their innate creativity. These are positive aspects of the throat chakra.

- Making good use of their imagination, trusting their hunches and intuitions, and continuing to learn and grow all the way through life. These qualities relate to the brow chakra.

- Nurturing and developing their soul by recognizing that they are interconnected with all life and establishing and maintaining contact with the Divine. This relates to the crown chakra.

If all seven of your chakras were balanced and in harmony, your life would be extremely happy. Fortunately, it's possible, and the angelic realms are prepared to help you achieve it.

The angels are also willing to help you release emotional blocks in your chakras. Here are some common reasons for blockages in the chakras:

Root chakra: Insecurity, self-doubt, unwillingness or inability to let go of the past

Sacral chakra: Selfishness, self-centeredness, apathy, difficulties in communicating with others

Solar plexus chakra: Low self-esteem, moodiness, feelings of hopelessness and powerlessness

Heart chakra: Difficulty in expressing emotions, insecurity, lack of empathy

Throat chakra: Frustration, impatience, hesitance, and inability to express innermost feelings

Brow chakra: Living in an unrealistic fantasy world, feeling overwhelmed and fearful, inability to accept the world as it is

Crown chakra: Rigidity, stubbornness, introversion, and alienation from others

Removing Emotional Blocks Ritual

This ritual with Archangel Michael enables you to eliminate any emotional issues you may have.

Think carefully about what you want to accomplish in the ritual. It can be helpful to write everything down, so you can refer to your notes during the ritual if necessary. As usual, set aside about an hour to perform it. Have a shower or bath beforehand and dress in clean, loose-fitting clothes. Place a straight-backed chair in the middle of the area where you'll be creating your magic circle.

Start by performing the Angelic Invocation of Protection in chapter 2.

Turn to face Archangel Michael and sit down in the straight-backed chair with both feet flat on the floor. Tuck your chin in slightly to ensure that your spine is straight. Rest the palms of your hands on your thighs and close your eyes.

Take several slow, deep breaths, and then talk (preferably out loud) to Archangel Michael. Tell him why you're holding the ritual. Ask him to help you balance your chakras, as your emotional blockage relates to whatever chakra it happens to be. If, for instance, you have problems expressing your emotions, ask Michael to pay special attention to your heart chakra. If you need to let go of the past, ask him to pay particular attention to your root chakra.

Focus your attention on your root chakra at the base of your spine. In your mind's eye, see it revolving and sense the powerful energy of the brilliant red color that emanates from this chakra. Visualize a ray of healing white light connecting the palm of Michael's right hand with your root chakra.

Wait until the ray of white light fades away, and then turn your attention to your sacral chakra. Again, visualize it revolving and sense the orange energy emanating from it. In your mind's eye, look at

Michael and see the ray of white light connecting his right palm with your sacral chakra.

Repeat with the other chakras. When you reach the chakra that relates to your emotional issue, visualize Michael in the usual way, but notice that the ray of light connecting the palm of his hand to your chakra is the same color as that radiated by the particular chakra. After this chakra has received enough of the colored light energy, you'll see the ray turn white again and remain as white light for the remaining chakras.

Once Michael has balanced your chakras, visualize them all, one at a time, and notice how much better you feel about every aspect of your life. You'll feel energized, motivated, and in total control. Thank Archangel Michael sincerely both for resolving the situation and for always being there for you whenever you need help.

Turn to face Archangel Raphael, and thank him for his love, protection, and guidance. Watch him fade from view, and then repeat this with Gabriel and Uriel.

Step outside the circle. Have something to eat and drink while thinking about the ritual you've just performed.

Self-Acceptance Ritual with Archangel Michael

Everyone on this planet is a mixture of often contradictory qualities that make up their personalities. No one is perfect, and to be truly happy and contented, we need to accept that we all contain both positive and negative sides to our natures.

Many people consider themselves to be charlatans who have achieved certain goals purely by luck rather than ability and hard work. Many people feel that although they have accomplished some important goals, it's not enough and never will be enough. Negative self-talk cripples many people. It's as if they're forever connected to someone who constantly criticizes them. It's no wonder that so many people don't like or accept themselves.

Archangel Michael is always available to provide protection and to keep you safe and secure in any type of situation, even when the enemy is the negative self-talk that comes from your own thoughts and feelings. Michael will also provide you with the strength and courage you need to accept yourself as the lovable person you are right now. He'll help you be true to yourself and stand up for what you believe is right. Most importantly, Michael will enable you to be kind, gentle, and loving to yourself in every type of situation. In other words, Michael will teach you to treat yourself in exactly the same way you'd treat your best friend.

Here is a visualization you can perform on a regular basis until any problems you have with self-acceptance have disappeared. You can do it whenever you have about twenty minutes of undisturbed time on your own.

Sit down quietly in a comfortable chair, close your eyes, and take several slow, deep breaths. Each time you exhale, silently say, "Relax, relax, relax."

Now shift your attention to a visualization of yourself sitting in a beautiful room. The furniture and furnishings are all beautiful, as are the paintings on the walls and the view from the open window. The sun is shining and you can hear birds singing outside. You feel warm, safe, and protected inside this magnificent room. Several feet in front of you is a large, comfortable-looking chair. You know this chair is for Archangel Michael, the angel you want to talk with.

As you look at the chair, Michael suddenly appears and sits down on it. He smiles at you, and you feel his empathy and love surrounding you like an aura. You feel a sudden surge of emotion as you realize that one of God's most important angels has made time to come and help you.

"Thank you for coming," you say. Michael smiles, and you instantly feel totally relaxed as you realize that you can discuss anything at all with him. Suddenly, your words flow as you tell him about your life and the difficulty you're having with liking and accepting yourself. You give him several instances when feelings of this sort held you back or you failed to make a good impression. When you've told Michael everything you can about your concern, you thank him for listening.

You look into Michael's eyes and feel his incredible love and compassion for you and for all humanity. You hear his voice clearly inside your head, as he gives you advice on what to do. He tells you to be kind to yourself and others, to put yourself first, to let go of toxic people, to practice gratitude, to surround yourself with the people you love, and to let go of the past.

Michael raises a hand and tells you to start immediately. "When was the last time you were kind to yourself?" he asks. "What act of kindness are you going to do for yourself today?" "What are you grateful for?"

"Remember," Michael tells you, "Let go of the past. Nothing's gained by constantly reliving painful memories. Realize that your thoughts aren't real. If you find yourself dwelling on something negative from the past, tell yourself it's only a thought and let it go. Keep on doing this until it gives up and vanishes permanently. Now, do you have any questions for me?"

Ask questions about anything you wish and listen to Michael's answers. When you've finished, thank Michael sincerely and ask if you can call on him again whenever it's necessary. Michael will respond positively. Thank him again, say goodbye, and then notice that the chair Michael was sitting on is suddenly empty.

Spend as long as you wish thinking about the visualization and the answers you received. When you feel ready, count slowly from one to five, open your eyes, stretch, become familiar with the room you're in, and carry on with your day.

The next Angel of the Presence we'll work with is the kind, generous, and loving angel of healing, Archangel Raphael.

Chapter Six

How to Work with Archangel Raphael

Archangel Raphael is one of the most important angels in heaven. His most important interests are healing, communication, creativity, knowledge, science, travel, and young people.

Raphael has always been associated with healing and can be called upon for all forms of healing, including spiritual, emotional, mental, and physical healing. He can also heal relationships between two people, heal problems between two countries, and heal the wounds of humanity. He combines his expertise as a teacher, as well as healer, when he helps us learn from the self-imposed wounds we give ourselves through our own actions. In the process, Raphael also helps us to reestablish our connection with divine love.

You can contact Raphael whenever anything major goes wrong in your life. A relationship breakup, or losing a job, are good examples. Raphael will help you restore unity and balance to your life. Raphael will also help you if you ever feel that you've lost your connection with the spiritual side of your life.

Archangel Raphael is usually associated with the color green, the color of healing, growth, and renewal, which are all qualities associated with him as well. Green is also associated with the heart chakra, the center of love, compassion, and forgiveness. This is significant because Raphael is often depicted as a compassionate and caring figure who is eager to help those in need.

Archangel Raphael is sometimes associated with blue, yellow, gold, violet, and pink. Blue is a symbol of peace, tranquility, and protection, while yellow and gold are associated with divine power, illumination, wisdom, knowledge, and enlightenment.

Color Breathing with Archangel Raphael

Most people are aware of the effect that colors have on us. Red, for instance, is a stimulating and exciting color. Blue is calming and reduces tension and fear. Extroverts usually prefer warmer colors, while introverts are more likely to be attracted to the cooler shades. Colors have strong psychological effects that affect our minds and emotions.

Colors also possess healing qualities. At least four thousand years ago, the ancient Egyptians had color-healing temples at Luxor and Heliopolis. Archaeologists have discovered special rooms in these temples in which the rays of the sun were broken up to form rainbows. Patients would spend time in rooms that corresponded with the specific color they needed.[4] Color healing was also practiced in ancient China, India, and Greece.

Color healing went into decline in the nineteenth century, when doctors began focusing on the physical body at the expense of the mental and spiritual aspects of their patients, but today a technique known as color breathing is frequently used to reduce stress.

---

4. Reuben Amber, *Color Therapy: Healing with Color* (Santa Fe: Aurora Press, 1983), 54–55.

Here is a useful color breathing exercise that you can use to make contact with Archangel Raphael.

Sit down comfortably with both feet flat on the floor, and close your eyes. Mentally scan your body, and consciously relax any areas of tension you find. If you've had a stressful day, for instance, you may notice that your shoulder muscles are tense. If so, roll your shoulders and allow them to drop down to release the tension.

When you feel reasonably relaxed, bring your attention to your breath and notice how it naturally starts to slow down as you relax.

Once your breathing has become slow and rhythmic, visualize yourself surrounded by a beautiful, pure white light. Each time you inhale, fill your lungs with pure divine energy, and each time you exhale, visualize yourself expelling negative thoughts and energies.

Enjoy the white energy for about a minute, and then allow it to gradually change into a perfect, pure gold color. Once the white light has turned completely golden, inhale as much of the beautiful gold energy as you can. Hold your breath for several seconds and then let it out slowly.

Take two more deep breaths of gold energy. Next, visualize the gold turning into the most beautiful green that you can imagine. Wait until you feel completely surrounded by the gorgeous green, and then take three deep, energizing breaths of green energy, holding each breath for several seconds before exhaling slowly.

Allow the green to turn back into the beautiful, pure, white light that you started with.

Enjoy the feeling of the gold and green energy in every part of your body, and then ask your guardian angel to ask Archangel Raphael to join you.

You'll notice a subtle change in the energies around you as Raphael arrives. Say hello as soon as you sense Raphael's presence, and then ask for help with whatever you need. Raphael is friendly and easy-going, and you'll enjoy the conversation, no matter what you discuss.

Thank Raphael sincerely once the conversation is over. Raphael will have probably told you to call on him whenever you need help or advice. If he hasn't, ask him if you can call on him again. As he has your interests at heart, he will always respond positively. Once he has left, thank your guardian angel, too. Relax and think about the session you have just had. When you feel ready, wiggle your toes and fingers, slowly count up to five, and open your eyes.

I always use gold and green when performing this exercise because Raphael's colors are yellow, gold, violet, pink, and green. You might prefer to replace gold with one of the other colors. Since green is a healing color, you should always use it when performing this visualization. Emotional and spiritual healing are important even when we feel perfectly well physically.

Rainbow Breathing with Archangel Raphael

Rainbow breathing is similar to color breathing, but the main difference is that you absorb the positive aspects of all seven colors of the rainbow. You can do this exercise on its own or incorporate it with the chakra exercises in chapter 5.

Start in the usual way by sitting down comfortably with your arms and legs uncrossed. Close your eyes and take several slow, deep breaths to relax your body. Mentally scan your body to see if any areas need special attention to help the muscles relax. When you feel totally relaxed, ask your guardian angel to join you.

Explain to your guardian angel that you would like Archangel Raphael to help you gain all the positive energies of a rainbow.

Visualize a pleasant outdoor scene in your mind. You can choose anything you like as long as there's a rainbow in the picture. You'll become aware of Archangel Raphael's presence as soon as he arrives.

Your guardian angel must have told him what you want to do, as he immediately tells you what a positive experience it is to walk through a rainbow.

You find yourself walking along a path that leads to your rainbow. Raphael holds one of your hands, and your guardian angel takes the other. The rainbow seemed far away but it takes only a few moments for the three of you to walk to the end of it.

Without pausing, you walk into the rainbow and are immediately surrounded by the most beautiful red color you've ever seen—it's warm, vibrant, stimulating, and energizing. You feel full of vigor and excitement as the red energy flows into every cell of your body. Archangel Raphael gently squeezes your hand and says, "Whenever you feel totally exhausted, visualize this and breathe in red energy to revitalize yourself." He gently squeezes your hand again, and you walk out of the red section of the rainbow and into the orange.

The orange color that surrounds you instantly enlivens your body, mind, and spirit. You feel cheerful, and your mind is full of positivity and new ideas. You also feel a strong sense of peace and love for all life. Archangel Raphael gently squeezes your hand again. "Don't forget," he says, "that orange is a healing color that can heal your body and mind." He squeezes your hand again, and you move into the yellow section of the rainbow.

As you become surrounded by yellow and breathe in pure yellow energy, your mind feels stimulated and full of positivity. You sense undeveloped talents and think of activities you never completed because something new came along to replace them. You want to share your ideas with friends before you forget them—your mind is teeming with creative thoughts. Again, Raphael squeezes your hand. "Breathe in yellow when you need new ideas," he says. "Yellow stimulates the mind." You take a few more steps and find yourself surrounded in pure green.

As you absorb green energy into every molecule of your body, you become aware of a sense of balance, harmony, peace, and well-being. You notice your body is free of tension. You realize now more than ever before that life has a purpose and you need to balance your physical and spiritual needs to achieve total happiness. You understand that hard work and organization are necessary to achieve your goals. Raphael squeezes your hand. "Green is the color of renewal," he says. "When your body, mind, and spirit need healing, inhale green energy."

You take a few more steps and find yourself totally surrounded by the most vibrant blue you've ever seen. You feel relaxed and stimulated at the same time. You have a desire to expand your horizons and become the person you're meant to be. Raphael squeezes your hand and says, "When you need to feel calm and secure, breathe in pure blue energy. It soothes the mind whenever you feel upset or experience mental strain."

You have a strong sense of the duality of your makeup as you leave the blue energy behind and step into the indigo. Your intuition seems to grow inside you and gain in strength. Although it used to seem hopelessly idealistic, you now want to see justice, tolerance, and fairness in everything you do. You want to help others to the best of your ability. Raphael squeezes your hand. "Indigo is love," he says. "Love in all its different forms and with everyone you interact with. Visualize this scene and breathe in love as often as you can."

You stop and look all around as you find yourself inside the violet ray of the rainbow. You feel sensitive, aware, peaceful, and so spiritual that you can sense the love that the Divine has for you. You realize that you need time and a great deal of introspection to develop the insights and understanding you desire. Raphael lets go of your hand and envelops you in a hug. "This is just a glimpse of what's ahead," he says. "You are growing and progressing, and violet gives you a small taste of what's in store. Whenever you want to be reminded of your spiritual nature, bathe yourself in violet energy." He smiles, and leads the way out of the rainbow and back into the pleasant scene where you started.

Thank Archangel Raphael and your guardian angel. Lie quietly for a minute or two, thinking about your rainbow experience. When you feel ready, slowly count from one to five and open your eyes.

Healing Prayer with Archangel Raphael

Archangel Raphael is best known for his healing work, so it's not surprising that he's arguably the most invoked angel of all. Raphael is friendly and willing to help anyone who asks him for help.

You can pray in any way that seems right for you. If you've always knelt down and held the palms of your hands together in front of your face, you'll probably feel most comfortable doing that when praying with Raphael.

When you pray to the Divine, you're actually praying to an infinitely powerful force that is part of you. It's best to pray to this force as if you were an integral part of the Divine, which is in fact what you are. Because you're conversing with the Divine, you don't need to worry about the words you use. Any prayer from your heart will be the right prayer.

And in fact, you don't need to use any words at all in what's known as contemplative prayer. To perform this, enter into the desired state of mind and open up your heart and mind to the Divine. The famous American speaker, writer, and clergyman Norman Vincent Peale (1898–1993) called this "thinking about God."[5]

---

5. Norman Vincent Peale, *The Power of Positive Thinking* (New York: Prentice-Hall, 1952), 92.

Healing Prayer Example

Sit down quietly somewhere where you won't be disturbed. Close your eyes, and think about your need for healing. If you're asking for healing for someone else, think about that person.

Ask your guardian angel to join you, and explain why you need Archangel Raphael's help. You'll sense Raphael's presence the moment he arrives. Thank him for coming to your aid so quickly, and tell him about your health concern and need for help. Raphael will give you all the time you need.

When you've finished, sit quietly and wait for Raphael to respond, most likely as a thought or a sense of knowing that he is delivering your request to the Divine.

Thank Raphael and then ask him to help you open up your heart and mind to the Divine. Remain in this state for as long as you can. Thank the Divine by saying, "Thy will be done." Finally, thank Raphael and your guardian angel for praying with you.

When you feel ready, open your eyes and continue with your day with confidence that your prayer has reached the Divine.

We've now looked at Archangels Michael and Raphael. In the next chapter we'll work with God's most important messenger angel, Archangel Gabriel.

Chapter Seven

How to Work with Archangel Gabriel

Only two angels are mentioned by name in the Bible: Gabriel and Michael. The name Gabriel means "God is my strength." Archangel Gabriel is best known for being God's main messenger. It was Archangel Gabriel who visited the Virgin Mary and told her that she was going to give birth to Jesus Christ (Luke 1:26–38). Gabriel can help you in many ways. She'll provide you with guidance to help you work out what you should be doing with your life. She'll also provide guidance whenever you have an important decision to make, such as a major purchase, changing careers, starting a new relationship, or beginning a family.

Gabriel will help you develop spiritually and intuitively, interpret your dreams, and bring you messages from the Divine.

This angel also provides purification if you have been hurt mentally or physically, if you need to rid your body of anything harmful, or if you feel negativity in your home or work environments.

You can also ask Gabriel to help you let go of painful memories; remove doubts and fears; and enhance feelings of joy, positivity, and gratitude.

Gratitude

Gratitude is a positive emotion that involves being thankful and appreciative for what you have and what other people have done for you. Most people express gratitude from time to time but sometimes neglect to express gratitude for smaller things, such as when someone holds a door open for them or stops to let them use a crosswalk. "Thank" and "you" are two deceptively simple words that hold enormous power. You express this energy and effectively send out a blessing every time you express your gratitude by saying them. It's not surprising that according to a Gallup poll, Americans consider Thanksgiving Day the happiest day of the year, as it's the one day in which people stop thinking about what they don't have, and express gratitude for what they do have.[6]

Give Thanks

When you thank someone, you're saying that you value them and are expressing your gratitude for what they've done for you. It's a small act of kindness that costs you nothing. Most people don't get thanked as often as they should, and you'll be pleasantly surprised at how appreciative people are when you thank them. They'll receive a psychological boost that will stay with them throughout the day. It seems that many people have forgotten how to say it.

You can ask your guardian angel and Gabriel to help you think of people who deserve your thanks. It might be a neighbor who willingly gives help when needed. It could be someone at work who encourages you or a friend who is always willing to listen. Once you start looking, you'll be amazed at how many opportunities you have to say thank you.

---

6. Philip C. Watkins, *Gratitude and the Good Life: Toward a Psychology of Appreciation* (New York: Springer Publishing, 2014), 15–16.

Gratitude Prayer with Archangel Gabriel

Gratitude plays an important role in prayer. Whenever you thank the Divine for all the blessings in your life, you're expressing your gratitude. You can pray with Archangel Gabriel whenever you wish and wherever you happen to be.

For as long as I can remember, I've enjoyed praying with Gabriel close to a source of water such as a river, pond, lake, or the sea. I don't know when I started doing this, but it must have been because I knew that Gabriel looked after the element of water. My habit was reinforced when I read *Messages and Water from the Universe* by Masaru Emoto (1943–2014). Dr. Emoto was a pioneer in studying the effects that thoughts, emotions, and the environment have on water. In his book he wrote: "Words and phrases that are based on universal truths, such as 'thank you' or 'love' and 'gratitude' formed lovely symmetrical hexagons (on frozen water)."[7] You don't need to kneel beside your bed with your palms pressed together to pray. You can pray at any time at all and include any angels you wish to help you. When I pray, I prefer to close my eyes, but this isn't always possible. When driving a car or going for a walk, it's important that you pray with your eyes open.

You can call on Archangel Gabriel directly or ask your guardian angel to invite her to join you. I usually do the latter, as my guardian angel is intimately involved in everything I do.

Once you know Gabriel is with you, express your love and gratitude to her, and then ask if she'd deliver your prayer to the Divine. You might say something along the lines of:

> Archangel Gabriel, thank you for joining me today. I've been thinking about all the blessings in my life and

---

7. Masaru Emoto, *Messages and Water from the Universe* (Carlsbad, CA: Hay House, 2010), xi.

wanted to thank you for encouraging me to express my gratitude openly and honestly. Please help me overcome any doubts or fears I may have about doing this. Also, please help me let go of any painful memories, so I can live freely and enjoy a life full of peace, love, and harmony. Help me release all negativity and focus on the positive aspects of my life. Thank you for guiding, helping, and protecting me in everything I do, and for showering me with blessings.

Please carry my prayers to the Divine, and express my thanks for the gift of life, the beautiful world I live in, and for all the opportunities I have been given to lead a worthwhile, happy life. Please bless and look after all the special people in my life and help me to strengthen my faith. Thank you, God (or whatever name you prefer to use). Thank you, Archangel Gabriel. Amen.

Finish by saying goodbye to archangel Gabriel and thanking your guardian angel. When you feel ready, carry on with your day.

The Gratitude Angels

Gabriel, Cahatel, and Ooniemme are the three most important angels of gratitude. You can hold a Council of Angels (see chapter 2) with them whenever you wish. They'll give you many ideas to help you express and receive gratitude.

Cahatel is a member of the Schemhamphoras, a group of seventy-two angels found in Jewish scripture who bear the name of God. As well as gratitude, Cahatel (sometimes known as Cahathel) helps farmers to improve the quality of their crops, and is therefore considered an angel of abundance and prosperity. This blessing also provided farmers with abundance in their lives. Cahatel is a nurturing and protective angel who is concerned with the happiness and well-being of humanity.

Ooniemme is an excellent angel to thank when you feel grateful and whenever you wish to send a blessing to someone.

Angels of Gratitude Ritual

This ritual gives you an opportunity to thank the angels of gratitude for everything they've done for you. Ahead of time, think of some occasions in the past when you felt gratitude. You will need to have four chairs inside your circle of protection.

Start with the Angelic Invocation of Protection (see chapter 2).

Close your eyes and ask your guardian angel to invite Cahatel and Ooniemme to join you in the circle. While your angel is doing that, turn to face Archangel Gabriel and ask her if she'd please join you inside the circle.

When the three angels of gratitude have arrived, ask them to sit down on a chair. Once they've done that, sit down yourself. Your guardian angel will stand beside you, most likely resting a hand on your shoulder.

Smile at the angels of gratitude and tell them how grateful you are for all their help, not just for you but for everyone on the planet. Give them some examples of occasions that made you feel truly grateful. Tell them how motivating, healing, and grateful they make you feel.

Ask them to fill you with kindness, appreciation, and gratitude. Explain that you need this, as there have been occasions when you forgot to express your gratitude or didn't really realize the kindness that had been given to you until it was too late to say thank you. Sit quietly for a minute or two and feel every cell of your body being filled to the brim with positivity, love, and gratitude.

Ask the angels of gratitude to tell all the angels how happy you are that they are in your life and that although you don't always say it, you are truly grateful for everything they do.

Thank the angels of gratitude again and ask them to please bless everyone who has ever helped you.

Stand up and say goodbye.

Spend a few moments thinking about the ritual you've just conducted, and then dismiss the angels of protection. Slowly count to five and open your eyes.

In the next chapter, we'll look at the fourth of the great Angels of the Presence, Archangel Uriel.

Chapter Eight

How to Work with Archangel Uriel

Uriel is one of the four great archangels but is not mentioned by name in the canonical scriptures. However, he has always been considered just as important as his fellow archangels, Michael, Gabriel, and Raphael. He was mentioned by name in the apocryphal Book of Esdras: "The angel that was sent unto me, whose name was Uriel, gave me an answer" (2 Edras 4:1). The name Uriel means "Flame of God" or "Fire of God," and artists usually depict him with a flame burning on the palm of his hand. This flame's light illuminates the world so that we can see all the beauty that surrounds us in God's creation. In the first Book of Enoch, he is described as one of the holy angels who keeps watch over humanity, and is in charge of thunder and earthquakes (1 Enoch 20:2). According to the Book of Adam and Eve, Uriel is also the angel of repentance.

Uriel is archangel of Earth and acts as a channel between our world and the Divine. One of his tasks is to bring God's plan into the material world. Uriel is also known as the archangel of prosperity, as much of our wealth comes from the earth, such as crops, oil, gold, diamonds, and other minerals. Uriel is willing to help people who are self-motivated and are not afraid of hard work to progress financially.

Uriel is willing to help people remove all the roadblocks that are preventing them from achieving success. Uriel is quick to forgive people for their mistakes as long as they learn from them. He encourages hard work, thriftiness, and good money management. He enjoys acting as a mentor for people who aim high and are prepared to work to achieve their goals.

One of Uriel's many titles is Angel of Terror. Like the other archangels, he's prepared to use his power when necessary; when he does, he acts swiftly.

However, Uriel is also an angel of peace. Another important task of Uriel's is to help people release pain and trauma. He provides peace of mind and tranquility to those who need it.

As the archangel of prophecy, Uriel helps people develop their talents in this area. If you're interested in tarot or dream interpretation, for instance, Uriel will be keen to help you. Uriel is also more than willing to help people who use their talents at divination professionally. All you need do is ask him to join you when you conduct your divination sessions.

Uriel is also the archangel of knowledge and wisdom. He will help you learn quickly and effectively and make good use of the information. He provides light and clarity to help you understand and resolve problems. Uriel is also a good angel to consult when you need to make important decisions.

Wisdom

Knowledge is information that has been learned. Wisdom is the ability to determine or judge what is true or right. Wisdom is knowledge in action—someone who is wise will make good decisions based on knowledge, experience, good judgment, and common sense.

We all gain knowledge as we go through life, but not everyone makes good use of it. Wisdom is a vital skill that enables us to handle whatever occurs in the best way possible to achieve the results we desire. The wise person makes up their own mind rather than unthinkingly accepting the thoughts of others. They also accept others as they are and respect everyone they deal with.

Wise people think before they act, and if they're angry or upset, they delay making a decision until they've calmed down. They also think before they speak, as they know that words cannot be unsaid. They see the value in being kind, good-hearted, and quick to forgive, learning from their own mistakes themselves. They place importance on taking responsibility for their actions and don't try to put the blame for any mistakes on others.

Ask Uriel to encourage you to work hard to gain wisdom, success, and peace of mind.

Uriel Visualization

I've met many people who were concerned about working with Archangel Uriel, as they'd heard how his anger could cause earthquakes and tidal waves. Fortunately, Uriel is also an angel of peace; communicating with him is a joyful experience. You can conduct a visualization with Uriel for any purpose whatsoever, especially those involving his areas of expertise. For explanation purposes I've assumed you're calling on Uriel as you have a strong desire to grow in knowledge and wisdom.

Ideally, have a bath or shower before performing this visualization, and wear clean, loose-fitting clothes. Place a comfortable chair in the center of the area where you'll create your circle of protection. The chair should face east, and the room you're conducting the ritual in should be comfortably warm.

Start by performing the Angelic Invocation of Protection in chapter 2.

Sit down in the chair and make yourself comfortable. Close your eyes and take five slow, deep breaths as you relax your body in one of several ways. For instance, you could focus on your breathing and on each exhalation silently say, "Relax, relax, relax," until you feel completely relaxed. You could also tighten and then relax different muscle groups in your body or silently count down from five to one and then allow a wave of relaxation to pass through you. The method I prefer is a progressive relaxation. Although it takes longer than the other methods, the process is enjoyable and makes a good way to start the visualization.

Start by focusing on the toes of your left foot and will them to relax. Once they have, allow your foot to relax, and then let the relaxation drift up into your calf and thigh muscles. Repeat this with your right toes, foot, and legs. Once they're fully relaxed, allow the relaxation to drift up through your stomach, chest, shoulders, arms, neck, and head. No matter what method you use, once you've finished, mentally scan your body and focus your attention on any areas that are still tense until they let go and relax.

Once you feel totally relaxed, visualize yourself in the countryside. You're walking along a path halfway up a hill. The side of the hill is covered with luxuriant green grass, and at the bottom you can see a large field of ripening corn. A grove of tall trees is off to one side, and you can hear birds singing. You look upward and see several birds flying overhead. From far away, you hear the mooing of a cow. Several fluffy clouds appear to be dancing in the clear and beautifully blue sky. You notice a rainbow in the distance. It's a strange sight on this beautiful, warm, sunny day. As you watch the rainbow, it seems to float closer and closer to you. The colors are radiantly beautiful, and you marvel at the beauty of everything you see. You see a tall man walking toward you across the field of corn. As you watch, the man appears to float above the corn, and in seconds he's standing in front of you. You notice the rainbow has shrunk in size and looks like a large glowing aura around him. The man, who is several feet tall, gives you the most brilliant smile you've ever seen. He has dark, curly hair and a neatly trimmed beard. He's wearing brown and green clothes that make you think of the element of earth. You know you're in the presence of the great archangel Uriel, and you're so overwhelmed that you struggle to say hello. Uriel's smile widens, and he gently touches your shoulder. "It's wonderful to meet you," he says. "I've been interested in you for a long time, and it's good that we finally have time to really get to know each other." His deep voice sounds like music. Uriel looks around and indicates a spot of grass beside the path. "Let's sit down here and have a chat." He sits down and pats the grass beside him. You feel nervous and excited as you sit down beside him. "Tell me a bit about yourself," Uriel says, "and then we can talk about how I can help you." Much to your surprise, you find it easy to talk to Uriel. He smiles and nods his head every now and again as you tell him about your life and your hopes and dreams. Once you've done that, you reveal why you need his help. "I want to learn more and grow in knowledge and wisdom," you say.

"That's a worthy goal," Uriel says. "You may not know it, but I think you're a wise person already. Someone without any wisdom would never ask that question. Let me see…

"Wisdom comes from experience, so be curious and investigate everything that interests you. Maybe you could read a book or magazine article on a subject you don't know anything about. You could learn a new skill. Talk to strangers; you can learn something from everyone. Not everyone will want to talk, but you'll be amazed how many people will be happy to chat with you. Listen more than you speak, and think about the conversation afterward. Keep an open mind. Talk with people who have different viewpoints to you. Be empathetic with everyone.

"Take some risks. Make sure to do something new every day. It doesn't have to be much; it could be as simple as changing your routine. Maybe you could take a different route to and from work. Don't worry about any mistakes you make along the way. I hope you'll make many mistakes—you'll learn from all of them. If you do as much of this as you can, you'll gain knowledge and wisdom all the way through life. Don't keep it all to yourself, though. Make sure to share what you learn with others. Don't push your ideas on others, but whenever someone asks you for advice, give them the benefit of what you've learned. That's probably enough for one day. Please ask me any questions you wish. I'm here to help you as much as I can."

You gaze across the valley and marvel at the beauty that surrounds you. It's hard to believe that you're receiving advice and guidance from Archangel Uriel. He smiles and puts an arm around you as you ask him a question. Uriel seems to have all the time in the world, and you're able to ask as many questions as you wish. After Uriel has answered all your questions, you thank him sincerely and ask when you can contact him again. "I'm always here for you," Uriel replies. "You can call on me whenever you need me." He gently pats you on the back and stands up to leave. "I'll see you again soon." He takes a few steps, and then starts moving faster and faster. The rainbow over his head expands in size and keeps up with Uriel's fast pace. In a matter of seconds, Uriel has disappeared from view, and the rainbow has returned to its normal size.

You remain sitting in the countryside for a minute or two to process what you've experienced and learned. When you feel ready, return to your comfortable chair surrounded by the four great archangels. Become familiar with your surroundings, thank and dismiss the archangels, and open your eyes.

Remember to ground yourself after the visualization by having something to eat and drink before continuing with your day.

You'll probably want to make notes about your visualization afterward. Do this as soon as possible while everything is still clear in your mind. Don't worry if you can't recall everything. Uriel always has a great deal of information to impart, and you'll remember what he wants you to know and act on right away. You can ask him for more information when you perform the visualization again.

In the next chapter we'll interact with Archangel Metatron, one of the only two angels to have lived a life on earth as a human before being transformed into an angel.

Chapter Nine

How to Work with Archangel Metatron

Spiritual development is a way of life that brings many rewards. As you grow spiritually, you help the entire world because you're raising the level of universal consciousness. At times, you may feel that you're not progressing as quickly as you'd like but, in actuality, every step you make helps everyone. Metatron, one of the greatest angels in heaven, wants to help you develop spiritually.

People call on Metatron when they need to think deeply about any issue or want to make major changes in their lives. He also helps people gain confidence and self-esteem and enjoys motivating people into action. He helps people focus on what's most important in their lives, a task often, but not always, related to spiritual growth. Despite his power and reputation, Metatron is extremely approachable and often called upon by people who are trying to improve in their work or in their relationships with family, children, and partners. He is sometimes known as the "miracle angel" because people call on Metatron when they're desperate for help and need a miracle in their lives.

Develop Your Personal
and Spiritual Power with Metatron

Metatron is one of the most influential of all the angels and is always busy. However, his main interest is in the betterment of humanity, so he's willing to help anyone who's genuine and sincere.

Before you start, think of a few questions you'd like to ask Metatron. You might like to ask him how to avoid temptations that could affect your spiritual growth; one possible question is if you're feeling hurt, betrayed, or angry, you might ask for angelic help as well as what you can do to help heal yourself. You could ask him how to resolve some of your fears. If you're a Christian, you might like to ask, "What does God wish me to do with my life?"

This exercise will take at least thirty minutes to complete. In addition to time, you'll need a chair, a surface to write on, and pen and paper. You might like to light a white candle and place it at the back of your table. If you do this, make sure to have a container of water nearby, just in case an accident occurs. You might also like to place a crystal on your table. I usually use celestite or selenite, but you can use any crystal that appeals to you or relates to your questions.

I like to perform this exercise after performing the Angelic Invocation of Protection (see chapter 2) because the process of constructing the circle and interacting with the four great archangels not only surrounds me and my workspace with protection but also gets me into the right state of mind to focus on whatever it is I want to discuss with Metatron. Because Metatron is extremely powerful and authoritative, you can leave this first step out if you're short of time.

Ask your guardian angel to help you come up with suitable questions to ask Metatron. Have a conversation with your guardian angel and explain why you want to communicate with Metatron, including what you hope to achieve as a result.

Ask your guardian angel to invite Metatron to join you. You might prefer to call out to Metatron yourself. Many people prefer this approach but whenever possible, I like to involve my guardian angel in my rituals and exercises.

You'll sense when Metatron arrives, perhaps something as subtle as a slight change of temperature, a sudden gust of air, or even a pleasant scent. You might experience a tingling sensation in your body or simply a sense of knowing that Metatron has arrived. When you realize that Metatron is with you, thank him for coming to your aid.

Pick up your pen or pencil and ask your first question silently or out loud. Metatron's answer is most likely to come as a thought in your mind. Don't analyze or question whatever comes through. Write down as much of it as you can. Once you've done that, you can ask as many additional questions as you wish about what you've recorded.

Ask other questions if you had any, and write down Metatron's replies each time. When you've asked all your prepared questions, ask, "Metatron, what is the best thing I can do right now to enhance my spiritual growth?" Once Metatron has responded and you've written down his answer, sit quietly for at least a minute, as he'll often have some further words of advice for you. During this time, your guardian angel may have a further question or two that you can ask Metatron to answer.

Once you're sure that Metatron has finished, thank him sincerely and express your gratitude for his help and advice. Tell him that you'll contact him again soon and will let him know how you're getting on with your spiritual growth. Say a warm goodbye. You'll know instantly when Metatron leaves. Just as earlier, you'll notice or sense a subtle change.

Thank your guardian angel for being there with you. You might have a brief conversation about the exercise you've just experienced.

If you've performed this inside your circle of protection, thank and dismiss the archangels one at a time. Become familiar with your environment and take five slow, deep breaths before opening your eyes. If you didn't create a circle, simply count to five and then open your eyes.

As always, eat and drink something to help ground yourself as soon as possible after the ritual.

How to Access Your Akashic Records with Metatron

One of Metatron's main responsibilities is to maintain and look after the eternal archives, the heavenly records that list all the thoughts, emotions, and deeds that have happened since the dawn of time. Known as the Akashic Records, these archives contain knowledge about your soul and its journey through all your previous incarnations, your present lifetime, and even information about possible future lives as determined by your thoughts and actions in this lifetime.

The first written reference to the Akashic Records is in the Bible. After the Israelites had committed the grave sin of worshiping the golden calf, Moses accepted responsibility and asked to have his name removed "out of thy book which thou hast written" (Exodus 32:32). The records are also mentioned in the New Testament: "And I saw the dead, small and great, stand before God; and the books were opened, which is the book of life; and the dead were judged out of those things which were written in the books, according to their works" (Revelation 20:12). Edgar Cayce (1877–1945), the famous American clairvoyant and prophet, called the Akashic Records

"God's book of remembrance."[8] No one knows where the Akashic Records are kept. Theosophists believe they're stored in a nonphysical plane of existence. Other sources say they're kept in heaven. For the purposes of this visualization with Metatron, we'll assume they're kept in a beautiful library. You might prefer to visualize the Akashic Records in a completely different way; this visualization will work just as well if you use your own ideas about where they're kept.

There are many ways to access the Akashic Records, all of which start with relaxing the physical body and getting into the desired meditative state. Once you've done that, you'll be able to access the Akashic Records in any way you wish. Some people start with a prayer, others visualize the Akashic masters who look after the records, and many use the help of an angel to guide them. During the process, people visualize the library in different ways. Most visualize a magnificent library inside a building that looks similar to an ancient Greek temple that happens to sit on a cloud.

You'll need about thirty minutes of uninterrupted time for this exercise. I usually do this visualization in a recliner and cover myself with a blanket, as I tend to lose a few degrees of body heat during the process. If you don't have a recliner, use a bed or any comfortable chair. That said, be careful about using a bed; take care not to fall asleep once you become relaxed. I can't use a bed for that reason but don't have that problem with a recliner.

Before you begin, choose a specific question or questions you'd like to ask. Whatever you ask must be open-ended and specific to ensure you get all the information you need. You don't want to receive "yes" and "no" answers; it's better, for instance, to ask to see a scene from a past life that relates to your present life rather than,

---

8. Mary Woodward, *Edgar Cayce's Story of Karma: God's Book of Rememberance* (New York: Coward-McCann Books, 1971), 238.

"May I visit a past life?" Relatedly, it's a good idea to ask questions that are relevant to you right now. You could ask about what your purpose is in this incarnation, or what talents and skills you had in previous lifetimes that could be applied again in this lifetime to help yourself and others. You'll certainly receive information related to subjects you're only mildly curious about, but it's better to respect Metatron's valuable time.

Create the Angelic Invocation of Protection around the chair you'll be sitting in (see chapter 2). Sit comfortably in the chair with your arms and legs uncrossed. Take a deep breath, and close your eyes as you exhale. Pay attention to your breathing, and allow yourself to relax more and more with each breath you take.

Once you feel reasonably relaxed, forget about your breathing and instead mentally scan your body to see if you can find any areas that are still tense. Focus on them until they let go and you feel totally relaxed in mind, body, and spirit.

Tell your guardian angel that you would like Archangel Metatron's help to access the Akashic Records. While you're waiting for Metatron's response, think about some happy times from when you were young and life seemed full of adventure and exciting possibilities. You realize that you still have unlimited potential, and in your mind's eye you can look back and see glimpses of your many, many past lives. You can also look forward and see all the future lives you haven't yet experienced.

You return to the present as Metatron arrives accompanied by your guardian angel. Metatron is extremely tall but has a warm, friendly smile and seems excited that you want to examine your personal file in the Akashic Records. He asks for your full name and date of birth, and then looks up and raises one arm. Instantly, you're surrounded with a pure white light—all you can see is Metatron and your guardian angel. You can hear Metatron asking to see your personal Akashic Records so you can gain all the information you need to make as much progress as possible in this incarnation.

The white light quickly dissipates, and you find yourself inside a beautiful library. Metatron indicates a table and chairs for the three of you to sit down. Completely covering the tabletop are files that you realize all relate to you. Many relate to previous lifetimes, some deal with the present, and the others contain information about possible future lives.

"What is your first question?" Metatron asks. As you ask your question, you sense a strong beam of golden light reaching downward from the top of the library and entering your body at the top of your head. You instantly feel it touch your heart and somehow know the answer to your question. Metatron smiles at you. "Do you have any questions about this matter?" he asks. You shake your head. "In that case, please ask your next question." Again, the answer instantly comes to you from your heart. You continue asking questions until you have all the information you need. Occasionally, you might ask for more information, but most of the time the answers contain everything you want to know.

Metatron senses when you've absorbed enough information. He looks upward again. "Please close (your name)'s records. Thank you." Instantly, all the files on the table vanish, and you notice the golden light has gone as well. Metatron takes you by the hand. "You can return any time you wish," he says. "But for now, let's take you home."

Your guardian angel takes your other hand, and the three of you walk outside. You catch a quick glimpse of a magnificent, radiantly white building sitting on a cloud. All three of you jump off the cloud, and you're immediately back home.

Metatron gives you a few moments to adjust and then says goodbye. "Thank you so much," you say. "You've helped me enormously." Metatron smiles again. "I'm happy to help. Ask your friend to find me and I'll be with you right away." In less than a second, Metatron fades away. You now turn to your guardian angel. "I've got a great deal to think about," you say. "Thank you very much for all your help." Your guardian angel hugs you and laughs. "I'm always here for you."

You smile as you recall the experience you've just had. When you feel ready, you count to five and open your eyes. Dismiss the four great archangels who have guarded your circle, and after grounding yourself with something to eat and drink, carry on with your day.

Now that we've spent time with five of the most important archangels, we'll start looking at some of the other angels who specialize in helping people deal with specific areas of life. In the next chapter we'll meet the angels of love.

Chapter Ten

How to Love Others and Yourself

Friendship occurs when two people enjoy spending time together and have positive thoughts and feelings for each other. Love takes this a step further and involves a strong sense of affection, tenderness, responsibility, trust, and commitment. Love comes in many forms but there's usually also a strong element of sexual attraction in romantic love.

Love is a complex mixture of emotions and behaviors that enhance our lives and frequently make life worth living. Love involves devotion, commitment, attraction, trust, and passion. When two people are deeply in love, they experience a wide range of positive emotions such as happiness, excitement, elation, and a sense of well-being. Love keeps people attached and committed to each other, even if the sexual element of the relationship gradually declines.

Love is a choice, too. It takes work—and often a great deal of it—to sustain a relationship. You choose love every time you focus on communication, intimacy, and trust in the relationship. Your actions and the actions of your partner determine whether or not the relationship will be a long-lasting one. Consciously (or not) you make this choice every day.

Although friendships and partnerships are important, perhaps the most important relationship in your life is the one you have with yourself. After all, loving yourself means accepting yourself as you are, recognizing your self-worth, and not living up to anyone else's expectations.

Fill Yourself with Love

No matter what's happening in your life, you can fill yourself with love. In fact, you're already full of love—your essential nature is pure love. It's an integral part of you, and you've always possessed it. Sadly, most people look for love outside themselves rather than within. Here are some ways to recognize and appreciate the love you have inside.

Practice forgiveness (see chapter 12). People who do this are happier, more optimistic, and more loving than people who hang on to their resentments and grudges. Forgive yourself, too. Every person on the planet makes mistakes. Take responsibility for what happened, make amends if possible, forgive yourself, and then let it go. There's nothing to be gained by holding on to painful thoughts for the rest of your life.

Do something every day that makes you feel good. It doesn't need to be the same thing every day, nor does it need to require much effort—it could be as simple as watching a favorite TV show, relaxing in the sun, or spending a few minutes talking to a friend.

Helping others is one of the best ways to help yourself. Every time you help someone, you receive more in return than you give.

Be kind to yourself. Most people are harsher on themselves than they'd ever be to someone else. Stop criticizing yourself, or putting yourself down. At any moment, you're doing the best you can, and that is enough. You are worthy of the very best life has to offer.

Be more loving. Send loving thoughts to everyone you know, and then start sending similar thoughts to people you don't know. These might be strangers you happen to see for just a few moments, as well as politicians, celebrities, and other people you see on TV. The more love you give out, the more love you'll receive back in return. Remember to send loving thoughts to pets, plants, favorite places, interests and passions, and anything else that's important to you.

Communicate with your guardian angel every day. Your guardian angel knows you better than anyone and will help you regain your love for life whenever you're feeling low. Your special angel is always with you, so you can enjoy a conversation together whenever you wish. If other people are around, you can speak silently and enjoy a private conversation at any time, no matter where you are or what you're doing.

Self-Care

Self-care is any action done deliberately to nurture and take care of yourself. It's vitally important for your physical, mental, emotional, and spiritual health, so make sure that every aspect of your being is receiving this valuable form of love. After all, it's difficult to help others when you're not looking after yourself. Self-care builds resilience, promotes well-being, provides joy, and creates feelings of happiness and worthiness.

Physical self-care involves feeding yourself with good-quality healthy food, exercising regularly, learning ways to reduce stress, and making sure that you receive enough sleep. Avoid illicit substances and be careful with alcohol. You also need to take care of yourself physically with regular checkups and by following your medical professionals' advice. Lelahel, Melahel, Raphael, Suriel, and Zuriel are all angels you can call on whenever you need help you with physical self-care.

Mental self-care involves being kind and gentle with yourself, paying attention to your thoughts and focusing on positive thoughts as much as possible, practicing forgiveness and kindness, and keeping your brain stimulated by learning all the way through life. Rehael and Zuriel are two angels you can call on for this; they specialize in working with people's guardian angels to enhance mental self-care.

Emotional self-care involves paying attention to your emotions and handling them to the best of your ability. Talking things through with a close friend, writing in a journal, meditation, and doing something you enjoy are all good ways to handle difficult feelings and emotions. Balthiel, Chamuel, Gabriel, Lahabiel, and Uriel are all specialists in emotional self-care and are always willing to help you.

Spiritual self-care involves nurturing your soul, and doing anything that helps you find meaning, comfort, and inner peace. This could be a religious practice, meditation, walking in nature, visiting sacred places, and helping others. You can call on any angel, especially your guardian angel, for spiritual self-care. Angels who specialize in this include Asmodel, Balthiel, Elemiah, Haamiah, Hariel, Jegudiel, Melchizedek, Micah, Pahaliah, Sachiel, and Sandalphon.

Social self-care involves everything we do with others, such as spending time with family and loved ones, connecting with friends, conversing with acquaintances and the people who serve us, complimenting people when they deserve it, and volunteering to help others. There are many angels who'll be delighted to help you with social self-care. These include Amnediel, Anael, Cambiel, Chamuel, Charmeine, Chavakhiah, Gabriel, Haaiah, Hanael, Jeliel, Mebahel, Raguel, and Verchiel.

How to Create More Love within Yourself

Many people who've experienced difficult relationships blame themselves for everything that went wrong; because they're consumed with negative thoughts, they find it hard to gain a positive perspective on life again. This negativity effectively destroys their sense of self-worth and makes it difficult for them to love themselves, let alone anyone else. Fortunately, the angels of love are keen to help anyone struggling with this type of negativity learn to appreciate themselves for who they are. They encourage them to be kind and gentle to themselves and to nourish themselves every day with good food, exercise, and positive interactions with good friends and loved ones. The angels can encourage us to accept ourselves as we are and to realize that we can love and be loved, even though (like everyone else), we aren't perfect and will make mistakes at times. The first step is learning to love ourselves again, a good starting point for building good, loving relationships with others.

The main angels of self-love are Gabriel, Michael, and Chamuel.

Archangel Gabriel provides guidance and purification. Gabriel also helps people recover after relationship breakups, and encourages people to be patient and allow enough time for healing to occur.

Archangel Michael helps people feel safe, which is vitally important for anyone who has been hurt or damaged in previous relationships. In a safe environment, we are enabled to let go of the past and become ready to allow love into our lives again. Archangel Michael also helps people gain confidence and self-esteem, something that's necessary for most people who have been badly hurt in relationships.

Chamuel, the archangel of unconditional love, helps people learn to love again. This includes self-love as well as romantic relationships. Chamuel encourages people to move forward and is willing to help us find a romantic partner when we feel ready.

Self-Love Ritual with Archangel Chamuel

You can perform this ritual whenever you wish. If possible, choose a place where you're surrounded by beauty, such as a park, a beach, or somewhere out in the country. It could just as easily be in a beautiful room surrounded by things that you love. I love books, so a library would be a good place for me to perform this ritual. If you can't find somewhere suitable, all you need do is close your eyes and think of the most beautiful place you can. It could be a place you've been to or a beautiful scene you've constructed in your mind.

Spend a few minutes enjoying the beauty that surrounds you. Pay attention to anything that captures your attention—the movement of clouds, the sound of birds, the beauty of something in the landscape, or the sensation of a gentle breeze on your cheek. If you're indoors, become aware of any sounds or smells you can sense. Enjoy looking at some of the items you love in the room. Thank Archangel Chamuel for all the beauty in your life.

When you feel ready, close your eyes, and take a few slow, deep breaths. Think of something that you appreciate about yourself. It could be anything: your intelligence, hair color, empathy, or skill at skateboarding. Once you've decided what it is, tell yourself that you're grateful for whatever it happens to be.

Think of something else that you appreciate, and express gratitude for this gift. Repeat this as many times as you can.

When you run out of things you appreciate about yourself, ask Archangel Chamuel to join you. Visualize him walking toward you with a huge smile on his face; he's obviously thrilled to join you. When he gets close enough, he hugs you for a few moments before stepping back and beaming at you. Tell Chamuel everything you appreciate about yourself and ask him if there's anything else he can add to the list.

Chamuel names something positive that he sees in you and gives you time to ask yourself if you recognize and appreciate that quality in yourself. Chamuel immediately notices anything you have difficulty accepting. Chamuel might say, for instance, that you are a lovable person. If you hesitate or appear doubtful, Chamuel will give you an example of a time when you exhibited that quality.

Chamuel suggests other qualities that you should appreciate and amplifies them if necessary.

Finally, Chamuel takes you by the hand and walks you through the area you are performing the ritual in or the imaginary scenario you constructed. He pauses frequently to point out objects of beauty that you may not have noticed on your own. It might be a particularly striking flower, a drop of dew on a blade of grass, or the song of a bird. "Isn't this world gorgeous?" he asks. "If you remain alert, you'll find there's beauty everywhere, even in the unlikeliest of places. There's beauty inside you, too. Many people love you because of your innate beauty. You are perfect inside and out. You used to love yourself once, and you'll love yourself again. Once you recognize all the good, positive qualities you have, you'll start seeing everything, including yourself, in a new light. Your love for yourself and for all living things will become a positive force for good in the universe. You are here for many reasons, the most important of which is love, starting with yourself." Chamuel smiles at you, and you feel every cell of your body responding to it. You smile too. "Call on me again soon," Chamuel says. "Let's do this ritual again and again until you're loving yourself every moment of every day." Then he fades from view.

Stay still and silent for a minute or two until you feel the time is right to slowly count from one to five and open your eyes again.

You'll experience the benefits of this ritual right away, and Chamuel's positivity and love will remain with you all day. Continue doing the ritual for as long as necessary, and remember to perform it every now and again to give you a boost of positivity and love.

Angels of Love

Many angels specialize in love (see appendix) and are ready to help you attract and enhance relationships. They're also keen to help you resolve any problems you may have in matters of the heart. Your life becomes richer and more spiritual every time you choose to love others. Whenever possible, demonstrate that love in small and large ways.

Archangel Michael provides guidance, protection, security, and advice in all types of situations. He is often called upon to help people with their relationship problems.

Archangel Raphael provides healing to restore the heart and soul after relationship breakups and attracts honesty and loyalty in future relationships. Raphael is sometimes known as the angel of marriage.

Archangel Uriel provides peace and harmony for people in volatile relationships. The name Uriel means "Flame of God," and this flame heals and purifies the heart. Uriel also encourages honesty and loyalty between the two people in the relationship.

Archangel Raguel provides peace, harmony, and cooperation when otherwise good relationships are struggling. People who are serious about finding a partner can call upon him for help.

Archangel Chamuel provides forgiveness, tolerance, understanding, and unconditional love. Chamuel brings peace to troubled relationships and is also interested in helping you to love yourself.

Archangel Jophiel helps provide inspiration, beauty, and joy to all relationships. Jophiel also helps people see the beauty inside themselves and start loving themselves again.

Anael has always been associated with love and affection, which may be why this angel is the most frequently invoked of all. Anael is willing to help in any matters involving love, affection, sexuality, peace, harmony, forgiveness, and inner peace. Austrian philosopher and spiritual teacher Rudolf Steiner (1861–1925) believed Anael was one of the seven great archangels. Anael is a member of the Sarim and is chief of both the Order of Principalities and Virtues.

Throughout history, people have wondered about the purpose of life. Is life simply a random, sometimes cruel waste of time, or are we living in this time and place for a reason? Fortunately, there are specific angels who can help you find meaning and purpose in your own life. We'll meet them in the next chapter.

Chapter Eleven

How to Find
Your Purpose in Life

The happiest people in the world know what their purpose in this lifetime is. Everyone has a reason or purpose for being here, although it often isn't easy to work out what it is. Some people instinctively know what they're here to do, and it usually involves developing a particular talent or skill they were born with. Other people decide early on in life what they want to do and then pursue it. Before he was a teenager, my father decided that he wanted to become a doctor and ultimately achieved that goal.

We're all here to learn lessons; for many, that itself is their life purpose. Those lessons might be about kindness, responsibility, love, or some other area of life. Many people think their purpose in life relates to work and career, but this isn't necessarily the case. I've met many people whose purpose in life was to be a parent, and they find great satisfaction and fulfillment in doing the best job they can at that. Many people find their life purpose in helping others in their community, often on a voluntary basis. They may coach junior sports teams or become involved in charitable groups who help young people, the elderly, or animals. Some people find their life's purpose in something they're passionate about, such as art or music. They may never become famous or even make a living out of their passion, but they're still pursuing their life's purpose.

One of the happiest people I know works as a caregiver for people who are intellectually handicapped. Although the work is hard and often thankless, she loves it because she knows her purpose in this lifetime is to care for others. The biggest clue to what your life purpose may be is to look at what you love doing and what you'd love to do.

While I was growing up, I was fortunate enough to be taught by a few teachers who brought the best out of me and made me want to learn. Their life purpose was to impart their wisdom and knowledge to others.

I worked as an entertainer for many years and know many people who are following their life purpose of bringing joy, laughter, and happiness to others. This may sound frivolous compared to someone whose purpose in life is to be a brain surgeon, but actually it's not: What could be more important than bringing a few moments of fun and enjoyment to someone who is suffering or in pain? Every purpose is important.

Your purpose in life is unique to you. Even if you never made any effort to find out what your purpose is, you'll still fulfill it because the necessary drive to achieve it will come from your soul, and you'll receive constant encouragement from your guardian angel.

Although you can lead a happy and outwardly successful life without knowing what your life purpose is, there are many benefits to finding it. Once you're following your soul's purpose, you'll lead a more meaningful life and feel happier and more fulfilled. You'll have a clear sense of direction and know what to focus on to help your development. You'll know why you're here and what you were born to do with your life. Knowing your purpose in life doesn't necessarily make your life easier, but you'll recover from setbacks more quickly and will be overall happier once your inner self harmonizes perfectly with your outer life.

Angels and Your Purpose in Life

There are five angels who regularly help people learn what their purpose in life is: your guardian angel, Archangel Gabriel (see chapter 7), Archangel Uriel (see chapter 8), Raziel, and Zadkiel.

Your guardian angel knows you better than anyone and is the first angel to contact if you're wanting to learn your purpose in life. Your guardian angel will remind you of your strengths, and may remind you of talents and skills that you haven't developed yet.

Raziel means "Secret of God." Raziel is said to be a member of the cherubim, a prince of the choir of Thrones, chief of the Erelim, and a member of the Sarim, the angel princes of heaven. An old legend says that Raziel felt sorry for Adam and Eve when they were banished from the Garden of Eden. He gave them the Book of the Angel Raziel, which contained all the knowledge of the universe and enabled them to survive and make a life for themselves outside the garden.

Raziel has a strong interest in magic and knowledge and is an excellent angel to contact whenever you're faced with imponderable questions, such as what your purpose may be in this lifetime. Raziel also enjoys helping original thinkers to develop their ideas. (More information on Raziel appears in chapter 15.)

The name Zadkiel means "Righteousness of God." Zadkiel is one of the most powerful angels in heaven and is said to rule the fifth heaven. He is the Angel of Divine Justice and one of the seven archangels named by Pseudo-Dionysius in the early years of Christianity. He's a planetary angel who rules the planet Jupiter. Because of the expansive nature of this planet, Zadkiel provides abundance, benevolence, compassion, forgiveness, good fortune, happiness, mercy, and tolerance. As the Angel of Divine Justice, he is also one of the best angels to call on if you experience financial or legal problems. He can also help you discover the purpose of your current lifetime.

Reflecting Meditation with Archangel Gabriel

This meditation could be described as reflective daydreaming; all it entails is sitting quietly with Archangel Gabriel for at least ten minutes. With practice, you might increase the length of time to thirty minutes. It involves commitment on your part, and should ideally be done every day.

At first glance, this meditation appears to be a simple exercise involving silent time with Gabriel. But what you're actually doing is getting to know yourself on a much deeper level than ever before. In these sessions with Gabriel, you'll gain insights into your life, your role in the world, and your purpose in being alive at this time in addition to enhancing your spiritual growth.

Set aside at least fifteen minutes of uninterrupted time. Sit down comfortably, close your eyes, and take five slow, deep breaths. Ask your guardian angel to ask Archangel Gabriel to join you.

Pay attention to your breathing until you sense that Gabriel has arrived. Say thank you and explain that you're going to spend ten minutes in total silence. Both Gabriel and your guardian angel will know that you're going inside yourself to gain spiritual information and learn more about your purpose in this lifetime.

Free your focus from your breathing and let your mind roam wherever it wants to. You may find that you immediately start thinking deep thoughts about life, but you may just as easily find yourself thinking about what you're going to cook for dinner. Your thoughts aren't terribly important to this exercise; the purpose of this reflective meditation is to become enfolded by the silence and to enjoy the feelings of peace and tranquility in your mind.

When the time you've allowed for the meditation is up, thank Archangel Gabriel and your guardian angel for sitting with you. Say goodbye and wait for about a minute before slowly counting to five, opening your eyes, and continuing with your day.

When you first do this meditation, you might find it helpful to set a timer to let you know when to end. With practice, you'll find it will no longer be necessary and you can automatically end the meditation at the right time.

Praying with Archangel Uriel

Archangel Uriel is happy to help anyone who is sincere and prepared to work hard to achieve their goals. Here is a short prayer to Uriel that will help you discover your purpose in this lifetime.

> Archangel Uriel, I'm calling on you today as I've not found it easy to discover my life's purpose. I realize everyone is different, and some people have always known what their purpose is, while others, like me, struggle to find out what it happens to be. I know that I may have a number of purposes, but I need your help to find out what my main purpose in this lifetime is. Would you please help me discover what I'm here for? What is the most fulfilling task I'm meant to accomplish in this incarnation? Please help me, Uriel. Thank you.

Life Purpose Ritual with Archangel Zadkiel

In this ritual, Archangel Zadkiel will help you write a life purpose message. Your life purpose message will gradually develop and expand over time, so it's likely to take more than one session. Consequently, allow at least thirty minutes each time you perform this. You'll need a table, a chair, a pen and paper. If you wish, you can decorate the table with candles, crystals, and any other items of a spiritual nature that appeal to you.

Create an Angelic Invocation of Protection (see chapter 2) around yourself.

Sit down in the chair and ask your guardian angel to invite Archangel Zadkiel to join you. You'll sense his aura of loving compassion and positivity as soon as he arrives. Although he appears to occupy your entire circle of protection, you don't feel hemmed in or restricted in any way.

Start by telling Zadkiel that you're seeking your purpose in life, and are going to write a message to help clarify what it is you need to accomplish in this incarnation. Briefly tell him about your life so far, including your successes and failures. Tell him about any ideas you've had about your life purpose along with anything else that seems relevant. When you've finished, pause, and wait for Zadkiel to respond.

Zadkiel tells you that you'll get better results by writing everything down. "Write down what you've told me," he says, "and then continue writing. I'll continue putting ideas into your mind."

Pick up your pen and start writing. It's a strange feeling: you write effortlessly, and the words come to you as if they're being dictated by someone else. After a time, the words dry up; Zadkiel says you've written enough for one day. He tells you to put your letter aside for a day or two before reading it. He tells you to think about what you wrote and write down any questions you may have about it. Once you've done that, he says, you should perform this ritual again.

You thank Zadkiel for his help and tell him you'll contact him again soon. You then thank your guardian angel and close the circle.

When you read what you wrote during the ritual, make any notes and write down any questions you might have. You're likely to be surprised at some of what you wrote and may even realize that information must have come from Archangel Zadkiel. You're likely to be impressed with what came through and realize that you're well on the way to determining your purpose in life.

Wait a day or two, and then when you're ready, perform the ritual again.

Start by performing the Angelic Invocation of Protection, and then invite Archangel Zadkiel to join you.

After he has joined you, ask Zadkiel your questions and listen carefully to his answers. Once you've done that, tell Zadkiel that no matter what your life purpose is, you want to be honest and ethical and treat people as well as you can. You want to be able to help other people recognize and celebrate their special attributes and talents. You also want to develop spiritually as much as you can.

You sense a feeling of warmth and comfort emanating from Zadkiel as you tell him this. "If that's what you want," he says, "I've no doubt you'll achieve it. Right now, though, it's time to start writing again."

You pick up your pen, and start writing. Again, the words flow easily, and you're amazed at how much you write before the flow of words stops.

You sense Zadkiel's pleasure in what you've done. "Do the same as last time," he tells you. "Put it aside for a couple of days before reading it. Once you've thought about what you've written, call me again."

You scarcely have time to thank Zadkiel before he disappears. You finish by thanking your guardian angel, and closing down the circle.

You can repeat this ritual for as long as it takes to gain a clear idea of your purpose.

An important part of any loving relationship is forgiveness. Couples who practice forgiveness are much more likely to stay together, and enjoy happier lives, than couples who hold grudges and refuse to forgive. We'll meet the angels of forgiveness in the next chapter.

Chapter Twelve

How to Work with
the Angels of Forgiveness

Everyone has been hurt at times by the words or actions of others. These events can be devastating when they occur, and many people compound this hurt by continuing to hold thoughts and feelings of anger, resentment, hate, and revenge, for months, years, and sometimes even decades after the event occurred. These people continue to punish themselves by reliving the event over and over again in their minds, long after the perpetrator has forgotten all about it. It's natural to feel angry when someone has deliberately or carelessly hurt you, but constantly feeding that anger hurts only you.

The remedy for this is to unconditionally forgive the person for what they did. It's a conscious decision to let go of the resentment, pain, and hurt that you've been holding on to. Forgiveness is a gift to the other person as much as it is a gift to you. Forgiving others is one of the kindest things you can possibly do for yourself.

Forgive Others

It can be hard to forgive someone, especially if the hurt involved bullying, humiliation, or a betrayal of trust. Some hurts may seem impossible to forgive. The victims of concentration camps or child-hood abuse are just two examples. Yet even in extreme cases like these, forgiveness is vitally important. It sets the people who are doing the forgiving free and enables them to move forward again with hearts full of love and compassion.

Forgiveness gives you peace of mind. In a very real sense, you're forgiving the person for your own sake. When forgiveness comes from your heart and soul, it's a joyful experience that enables you to eliminate all the bottled-up negativity that has been poisoning you for so long. Nelson Mandela (1918–2013), statesman and first president of South Africa, said: "Forgiveness liberates the soul. It removes fear. That is why it is such a powerful weapon."[9] Emotional scars are insidious and powerful enough to destroy much of the joy of life. Holding a grudge always hurts you but has little or no effect on the other person, who may have forgotten all about what occurred as soon as it happened. Forgiveness does not mean condoning what occurred. You don't necessarily need to forget what happened, either. In many cases, it might be impossible to do that. It also doesn't mean that you must reconcile with the person who caused you pain. What you are doing is letting go of the anger, bitterness, grudges, and hurt you've been carrying and replacing it with happiness and a new appreciation of all the goodness that surrounds you.

Dr. Christopher Peterson (1950–2012), formerly the Arthur F. Thurnau Professor of Psychology and Organizational Studies at the University of Michigan, wrote that the ability to forgive was possibly the most important factor in happiness: "Forgiveness has been described as the queen of virtues—that is, those who forgive are

9. Nelson Mandela, *Nelson Mandela: In His Own Words* (New York: Little, Brown and Company, 2003), 18.

much more serene than those who do not and display many other positive strengths."[10]

Forgive Yourself

Just as important as forgiving others is forgiving yourself. It's impossible to feel happy and positive when you're blaming yourself for something that you did months, years, or even decades ago. Remember that you're a human being, and everyone makes mistakes. We have all said and done things that we regret.

The first step is to acknowledge that you made a mistake and that you are responsible for any harm or hurt that your action created. If possible, apologize to the person you hurt. They may not accept your apology but will realize that you are trying to make amends.

There are many angels of forgiveness, including Adnachiel, Anael, Balthiel, Chamuel, Hariel, Jeremiel, Uzziel, Vasariah, Zadkiel, and Zaphkiel. If the matter is especially important, you might choose to consult with them all in a Council of Angels (see chapter 2). For Anael, see chapter 10. For Balthiel, see chapter 4. For Zadkiel, see chapters 11 and 16.

Adnachiel is an extremely positive and enthusiastic angel who enjoys working with people who are engaged in adventurous and pioneering activities. Adnachiel looks after Sagittarians and the month of November. He appreciates and bestows blessings on people who are kind, appreciative, and loyal. He encourages forward planning, to ensure that you live a stimulating and fulfilling life, both in the present, and in the future.

The name Chamuel means "He who seeks God." He is known as the archangel of peace, as he works tirelessly to create peace, harmony,

---

10. Christopher Peterson, *A Primer in Positive Psychology* (New York: Oxford University Press, 2006), 33.

and love in the world. He is also the archangel of compassion and unconditional love. He can be called upon for any matters involving forgiveness, tolerance, and understanding. Chamuel will help you in any situation where you need additional strength or are in conflict with someone else. Chamuel will help you find the beauty and love that surrounds you in the present moment, enabling you to live in the present. He gives people hope for the future, and helping people to forgive others is an important part of his work. He will also send love to the people you're forgiving.

Chamuel's colors are pink, orange, and light green.

Hariel is one of the seventy-two Schemhamphoras, a group of angels who bear the various names of God in the Jewish scriptures. He is also a member of the choir of cherubim. He is extremely interested in natural science. He also helps people appreciate beauty and the finer things of life. He has a strong interest in matters involving compassion and forgiveness.

Jeremiel's name means "Mercy of God." She helps people make positive changes in their lives, and heals matters that have been kept secret or hidden. Jeremiel's main work is as an angel of mercy, compassion, and forgiveness, but she also encourages people to make good life choices and steps in when people are involved in stressful and painful situations. She encourages people who are developing the spiritual and intuitive parts of their lives. She also helps people interpret their dreams. Not surprisingly, Jeremiel usually communicates with people in visions and dreams. Jeremiel's color is violet. (You can learn more about Archangel Jeremiel in chapter 16.)

The name Uzziel means "God's mercy." He provides faith, love, and hope when life seems grim and unfair. He works hard to teach people faith, hope, love, and forgiveness. According to the apocryphal Book of the Angel Raziel he is an archangel, and one of the seven angels who stand in front of the throne of God.

Vasariah is a member of both the Choir of Dominions, and the Schemhamphoras. He has a strong interest in justice and looks after lawyers, judges, and courts of law. He can be called upon to help in any matters involving justice, honesty, fairness, compassion, and forgiveness.

Zaphkiel is a member of the choir of Thrones and one of the planetary angels who look after the planet Saturn. Zaphkiel is willing to help in all matters involving passion, love, compassion, and forgiveness. He also helps people develop spiritually.

Chakra Forgiveness Exercise

This is a short exercise that sends forgiveness to every cell of your body. Ideally, you should do this while standing with your arms by your sides, and your legs slightly apart, but you can also perform it while sitting or lying down if necessary.

Close your eyes, and ask your guardian angel to invite whichever angel of forgiveness they think would be most helpful to you.

When you sense that the angel is with you, say thank you and ask for help in forgiving yourself for any misdeeds you may have intentionally or inadvertently done to hurt anyone else.

The angel places a hand on top of your head. You feel your feet becoming firmly rooted to the earth and experience forgiveness energy rising up both legs and into your root chakra. You instinctively know that this energy is pure gold in color. Feel it revolving in circles inside your root chakra, eliminating all negativity and filling your body with love and forgiveness.

The angel gently raises his hand and taps the top of your head. The golden energy immediately flows up to your sacral chakra, and you feel it again revolving in circles inside the chakra as it eliminates negativity and enhances feelings of joy and well-being.

Each time the angel gently taps the top of your head, the golden energy rises up to the next chakra until finally it reaches the crown chakra at the top of your head. You can sense the golden energy has reached and filled every cell of your body. You know that you have finally forgiven yourself and can start moving forward again.

The angel gives you a hug. As he does, you can sense the golden energy traveling down through your body to your feet and then into the earth. You feel full of love and happiness.

You thank the angel and your guardian angel. The angel squeezes you tightly for a moment and then releases you from the hug.

Remain standing with your eyes closed for as long as you wish. When you feel ready, slowly count from one to five, and open your eyes.

Forgiveness Council of Angels

Before performing this ritual, think about everyone who has ever hurt you in any way, at any time in your life. Recalling past hurts might be painful, but the purpose of this ritual is to release all the pain and let it go, not retraumatize yourself. Remember that you will have angels with you for the entirety of this ritual and can stop if things become too overwhelming.

Start by creating a magic circle using the Angelic Invocation of Protection in chapter 2.

Visualize yourself inside a bubble of golden light. Each time you inhale the golden light fills every cell of your body with spiritual energy. Each time you exhale the bubble grows larger until it fills your entire circle of protection.

Invite as many of the forgiveness angels in the appendix as you wish to join you. When performing this ritual, I always invite Archangels Jeremiel and Chamuel.

Once the angels are with you, thank them for helping you release all the hurt and pain, and enabling you to unconditionally forgive everyone who has ever hurt you. Tell them that you allowed your ego to take over and you no longer need to be right or choose to hang on to grudges—you want to lead a life full of happiness and love. Ask the angels to help you release all thoughts and feelings that could stand in the way of unconditional forgiveness. After this, pause for at least sixty seconds and enjoy the sensation of being surrounded and enveloped by total love. When you feel ready, say (preferably out loud): "I forgive everyone who has ever hurt me."

Ask Archangel Chamuel to help you send love to everyone who has ever hurt you. Say: "I now send love to everyone who has ever deliberately or inadvertently hurt me."

Ask all the angels to help you send the golden light of pure love to everyone in the world who needs it. Pause for about thirty seconds, and then thank the angels for doing this, and for helping you whenever you need it.

When you feel ready, thank the angels once more and say goodbye. Visualize the golden light fading from sight and thank Raphael, Michael, Gabriel, and Uriel for their help. Close the magic circle, slowly count to five, and open your eyes.

Self-Forgiveness Ritual with Archangel Jeremiel

You can perform this ritual as often as you wish. Although the process might be emotional, you'll definitely find it healing. Unlike other rituals, you can do this ritual when you already feel relaxed, no matter what you're doing. You could perform it while doing something you find relaxing, such as enjoying a warm bath or a cup of coffee, sitting outside on a summer's day, or taking a walk. You can even perform it in bed before going to sleep.

Start by consciously relaxing different parts of your body.

Once you recognize that you're physically relaxed, think about what you did and the harm you did to others. Turn your attention toward your pain.

Call on Archangel Jeremiel and ask her to surround you with her healing violet energy. Feel her love, warmth, and spirituality as it filters in to every part of your body and releases all the pain and hurt.

Thank Jeremiel for helping you to forgive yourself. Tell her that you've learned from the experience and will do your best to be kinder and more loving in the future.

Now ask yourself for forgiveness. When you do, feel it in every cell of your body.

Next, it's important to send love to yourself. It's difficult to send love to yourself when you're hanging on to negative energy. Forgiving yourself means becoming more loving, and sending love to yourself will feel natural and effortless.

Express your gratitude to Jeremiel once again, and send love to all the world.

Enjoy the sense of love and freedom this ritual has given you for as long as you wish. When you feel ready to return to your everyday life, count up to five, open your eyes, and stretch.

If you wish, you can perform the forgiveness council and the self-forgiveness rituals one after the other. If you do this, you won't need to relax before starting the self-forgiveness ritual, as the forgiveness council will have automatically helped you enter into the desired state of mind.

Forgiving yourself and others is an act of kindness you give to yourself that reduces negativity and stress, and fills you with love, compassion, and joy. Kindness is a vital part of leading a happy and worthwhile life, and there are special angels of kindness who'll help you attain it. We'll meet them in the next chapter.

Chapter Thirteen

How to Work with the Angels of Kindness

Kindness is the quality of being friendly, generous, and considerate. When someone is kind, they are compassionate and concerned for the welfare of others. Being kind means being willing to give your time and expertise to help people who need it. It also involves nurturing and caring for others. In its truest form, kindness is truly altruistic—it means giving to others without expecting anything in return.

Kindness is also a highly effective way to resolve almost any problem. It's hard to argue with someone who is being kind to you.

More importantly, kindness helps you see that everyone in the world is connected and we are all one. For many people, this realization is the first step toward spiritual growth.

It may seem hard to believe, but every time you're being kind to someone you also help everyone on the planet, as your good deed raises the level of universal consciousness. Even the smallest acts of kindness have a positive effect on the world.

Obviously, acts of kindness benefit their recipients, but it's just as true that kind people also gain from their actions. Helping others feels good, and kindness reduces stress, decreases blood pressure, raises self-esteem, improves moods, and enhances our relationships. Kind people also live longer.[11]

How to Bring More Kindness into Your Life

Despite the obvious advantages of kindness, many people fail to value it or ignore the benefits kindness can bring to their own lives. One reason could be the fast pace of life that leaves everyone with less time than they used to have. Self-centered people can take advantage of this by ignoring the needs of others to focus solely on what they want. Normally kind people might fail to stop to listen to the concerns of someone else because it takes time out of their already busy schedule, and they might be called upon to do something to help.

Fear could be another factor. Some people worry that when they express kindness, they might be considered weak or vulnerable. Worrying about others' thoughts or comments can make people hold back from being kind.

Self-centeredness and fear have always been with us, but our growing dependency on technology and social media has led to a dehumanizing effect on us. If a friend posts a sad or unhappy comment, it's easier to click a "like" or thumbs-up button rather than make contact and offer help.

People who are experiencing a bad time in their lives sometimes take out their feelings on others by being mean, discourteous, and rude.

Just recently I read an article which discussed the "me first" society we live in today. Kindness to others doesn't figure in this sort of world.

---

11. Steve Siegle, "The art of kindness," *Speaking of Health* (blog), Mayo Clinic Health System, May 29, 2020, https://www.mayoclinichealthsystem.org /hometown-health/speaking-of-health/the-art-of-kindness.

Fortunately, kindness is innate in most people, even if it can be forgotten at times. If for any reason you're finding yourself less kind than you used to be, remember that kindness is contagious. The best way to combat unkindness is to be as kind as you can, as often as you can.

Smiling, making good eye contact, and listening to others is a good way to start practicing kindness; you'll become more empathetic and kindness will quickly follow. Practicing random acts of kindness is another useful way to become kinder and can be as simple as passing a compliment or holding a door open for someone.

The angels of kindness are always there to help you become kinder both to yourself and to others.

Angels of Kindness

Your most important angel of kindness is your guardian angel. Gabriel is a busy archangel but can be called upon for kindness or any other matter, any time you need her. The other angels who have a particular interest in kindness are Haamiah, Hael, Lauviah, and Vasariah.

Haamiah belongs to the order of Powers. He is the angel of integrity and kindness. He protects people who seek the truth, and looks after people who are genuinely searching for spiritual knowledge. He can also be called upon to grant happiness to people in long-lasting relationships. Haamiah, Lauviah, and Vasariah are all members of the Schemhamphoras, a group of angels who bear the various names of God found in the Jewish scriptures.

Hael is an important angel of kindness, and is the angel to call upon when you want to send blessings to someone to thank them for their help or kindness.

Lauviah is said to belong to the order of Seraphim. He is also a member of the Schemhamphoras. According to the Jewish Kabbalah, he is a member of the order of Thrones. Lauviah promotes positive thinking and is considered to be an angel of kindness, joy, and happiness. You can work with him for recognition as well as success.

According to the Kabbalah, Vasariah is a member of the order of Dominions. He has a special interest in honesty, justice, and the law. Vasariah can be called upon for any matters involving kindness, fair play, and trustworthiness.

Lovingkindness Meditation

Some 2,600 years ago, Siddhartha Gautama, better known as the Buddha, is said to have taught a form of meditation known as *metta*. In the Pali language (in which many Buddhist scriptures were written), *metta* means loving/friendliness and kindness toward others. In this meditation, you will recite positive phrases for yourself, family, friends, difficult people, and ultimately, all living things. It's a highly effective way to cultivate unconditional kindness and compassion. It's also an excellent way to practice self-kindness, an aspect that many people overlook. I've found this ancient meditation to be even more effective when performed with the help of the angels of kindness.

All you need is a comfortable chair to sit in. Ahead of time, think of someone (or some people) you'd like to send positive wishes to. Set aside at least thirty minutes to perform the ritual. If possible, have a shower or bath beforehand and dress in clean, loose-fitting clothes.

Place your chair in the center of the circle you'll create facing east. Start by performing the Angelic Invocation of Protection in chapter 2.

Sit down in the chair and take five, slow, deep breaths, holding each inhalation for a few seconds before exhaling. On the sixth inhalation, visualize it flowing through your body to your heart, and feel your heart expand inside you. If necessary, continue sending your breaths to your heart chakra until you feel strong feelings of universal love emanating from it.

Now, shift your attention away from your breathing. Call on your guardian angel and explain that you're going to perform a lovingkindness meditation, and would like Haamiah, Hael, Lauviah, and Vasariah to join you. When they appear, ask them to stand in the four cardinal directions facing the four great archangels. Ask your guardian angel to stand close to you and either hold your hand or hug you.

Visualize yourself in your mind, sitting in your chair with your guardian angel beside you surrounded by a circle of angels of kindness and a circle of the four great archangels. Say: "May I feel safe. (Pause) May I be happy. (Pause) May I be healthy. (Pause) May I find peace." Think about the meaning of the words and how they make you feel. If you notice any positive feelings forming, associate them with their respective phrases, imagining them inside your heart chakra. Imagining them in this way will increase their effectiveness whenever you perform this meditation again. Let any feelings come and go. If you wish, you can repeat the phrases over and over again until you sense that every cell of your body has responded to the words.

Think of the person to whom you want to send positive wishes. Visualize this person sitting or standing directly in front of you. Say (preferably out loud): "May you feel safe." Pause for a few seconds, and say: "May you be happy." Pause again, and say: "May you be healthy." Finally, after another brief pause, say: "May you find peace." Hold those words in your heart and feel it expand. Ask the angels of kindness to strengthen your words and to send them to the person you're sending wishes to. Repeat this step as many times as you wish before moving on.

Ask the angels of kindness to surround you with positivity, kindness, and love. Wait until you feel their love in your heart and then thank them for their help. As you say goodbye, tell them that you'll be calling on them again soon.

Thank Raphael, Michael, Gabriel, and Uriel, and close the circle of protection.

Thank your guardian angel. When you feel ready, open your eyes, stand up, stretch, and have something to eat and drink before returning to your everyday activities.

You should feel invigorated, positive, warm-hearted, and loving after performing this meditation. The good thing about this meditation is that you can perform it as often as you wish. Even when you don't have time to perform the complete meditation, you can repeat the words as many times as you can, wherever you happen to be. For instance, you can say them when you're stuck in traffic or waiting for an elevator. You can even say them to yourself while walking through a crowded shopping mall.

This is the basic meditation. After you've performed this meditation a few times, you can extend it firstly by adding a few more friends, and then by adding neighbors, acquaintances, colleagues, animals, and ultimately everyone in the world. In fact, you can include the world itself—it needs lovingkindness, too. You can send wishes to groups of people rather than necessarily naming each person. When extending the length of this meditation, make sure to include people you don't like or have had problems with as well.

You can change the words to anything that resonates with you. Here are some suggestions:

- May I be confident.
- May I be more loving.
- May I be calm and relaxed.
- May I be free of pain.
- May I find happiness.
- May I feel full of joy.

- May I be sympathetic and understanding.
- May I be calm and relaxed.
- May my heart be filled with kindness and love.
- May I be healthy in body and mind.

How to Inspire Kindness in Others

Kindness is often spread by example. Whenever someone witnesses you performing a kind act, there's a possibility that they might be encouraged to do something kind themselves. It's wonderful to be able to instill kindness into one person, and there are a number of recorded instances of how a small act of kindness positively affected hundreds of people. In 2020, one man's random act of kindness of paying for the meal of the driver in the car behind him in the drive-through line at a Dairy Queen in Brainerd, Minnesota, motivated more than nine hundred other drivers to do the same thing![12]

Sadly, you're also likely to witness a great deal of deliberate unkindness as well. Drivers refusing to let other drivers change lanes is a common example. Bullying, insulting behavior, and name-calling are others. Gossip is often unkind.

It can be hard to know what to do when you experience unkindness yourself, or see it happen to someone else. If the unkind person seems angry and aggressive, it's usually better to remove yourself from the situation as quickly as possible.

If you know the perpetrator's name, you can ask your guardian angel to speak to his or her guardian angel about what the person has done. You can also ask the angels of kindness to send love and healing to that person.

---

12. "More than 900 cars 'pay-it forward' in random act of drive-through kindness," *BBC News*, December 9, 2020, https://www.bbc.com/news/world-us -canada-55254082.

If you don't know the person's name, ask the angels of kindness to send blessings to him or her. This may sound strange. Why would you ask angels to send a blessing to someone who has been unkind to you, or someone else? The angels will surround the person with love, and may help the person change their attitude toward other people.

It's not easy to remain kind, compassionate, and nonjudgmental when you experience unkindness, but returning unkindness with more unkindness is not a solution. When you fill your heart with kindness, and perform acts of kindness as part of your everyday life, you express your love and compassion everywhere you go. If you have any doubts, have a council meeting with the angels of kindness to ask them what you should do.

Whenever you're being kind, you're practicing a form of mindfulness. It's impossible to be kind if you're not living in the moment and focusing on the object of your attention. We'll discuss the angels of mindfulness in the next chapter.

Chapter Fourteen

How to Work with the Angels of Mindfulness

I was tempted to call this chapter "stop scrolling and live in the moment." Not long ago, I walked along a beach on a beautiful, sunny day and noticed that a large number of people were busy scrolling through their phones rather than enjoying all the beauty that surrounded them. When I mentioned this to a friend, he said he thought it was because people found it hard to relax for more than a few minutes and needed something to temporarily still the constant chatter going on inside their heads. It seems sad that in today's fast-paced world, people find it hard to slow down and simply enjoy the pleasures of the moment.

Living in the moment means letting go of the past, making the most of the present, and refusing to worry about the future. Many people spend much of each day ruminating about something that happened weeks, months, even many years ago. While they're doing that, they're living in the past, and are missing out on all the joys that the present moment offers. Other people constantly worry about the future. There's no point in doing that, as no one knows what the future holds for any of us. Obviously, we should learn lessons from the past, and make plans for the future. At the same time, we should make the most of what life has to offer us in the here and now. Our focus is best applied to the present moment, accepting the situation as it is, and refraining from judging anything as being good or bad.

Another name for living in the present moment is mindfulness. Researchers have discovered that living in the moment produces positive physical effects on the body such as reducing stress, lowering blood pressure, and improving sleep. Mindfulness can also help with mental problems such as anxiety, depression, eating disorders, and substance abuse.[13] In addition, practicing mindfulness produces chemicals in the brain that improve our moods.

Most people are controlled by their thoughts and act on them as if they were true. This can create huge problems, as we all have a tendency to inflate even slightly negative thoughts. Some years ago, I had a client who would lie in bed at night thinking about something embarrassing or foolish he'd done during the day. This memory would make him think of something that had happened a week ago, and this led him to another similar thought that had occurred a month or two earlier. After a few minutes, he was thinking of something bad he'd done when he was four years old. No wonder he couldn't sleep.

If we observe our thoughts and allow them to come and go without judging them, we gain control and start living in the present moment. Luckily, there are many ways to do this. Some we've already covered, such as kindness, gratitude, and forgiveness. Some other methods to help you make the most of the present moment appear here. You can do them on your own, but all of these experiences will be enriched if done with the help of your guardian angel.

---

13. Harvard Health, "Benefits of Mindfulness," HelpGuide.org, February 23, 2023, https://www.helpguide.org/harvard/benefits-of-mindfulness.htm.

Pause and look around the environment you're in. Focus on the sights, sounds, smells, and how you're feeling. If you're like most people, you're so busy in your own mind much of the time that you scarcely notice what is going on around you. Whenever a friend of mine goes on a walk, she sets a focus before she starts. One day she'll decide to focus on the different smells she experiences, on another day she may pay particular attention to the birdlife, and on yet another day she may pick up any litter she sees as she walks.

Walking with your guardian angel is a wonderful way to enjoy life in the present moment. Your angel will help you pay attention to where you are going, what to look at, and how to practice mindfulness while you're walking. When you start out on your walk, ask your guardian angel to join you after a few minutes. Your guardian angel is already with you, of course but will appreciate having special time with you to appreciate and enjoy the present moment.

Spend an entire day without worrying. Whenever you find yourself worrying about anything at all, gently tell yourself that you'll deal with the matter tomorrow. Close your eyes for a few moments and think about something that makes you happy. It could be happy times spent playing with your pet, vacationing with someone you love, or enjoying a meal with an old friend. By the time tomorrow comes around, many of the worries will have resolved themselves or won't seem to be as important as they were before. Ask the angels who help people overcome worry (Adnachiel, Caliel, Lauviah, and Michael) to stay with you during the day and be ready to encourage you to keep focused on all the positivity you have in your life.

A large percentage of the world's population dislike their work. A 2022 Gallup poll found that only 33 percent of workers felt engaged in their work, and 50 percent of all workers felt stressed on a daily basis.[14] Spend your next full day at work making the most of everything you can. Be alert, pay attention, and find joy in the smallest things. When you actively seek out happiness and enjoyment, you'll find it. It's a sad waste of your precious life if you enjoy yourself only on the weekends. Ask the angels of work (Cahetel and Menadel) to stay close to you and help you gain pleasure and satisfaction from your job.

Avoid multitasking. You can't live in the present moment when trying to juggle a number of tasks simultaneously. You'll achieve better results when you focus on completing one task at a time and as a bonus, make the most of the present moment as well. Ask your guardian angel to help you to focus and do one thing at a time. If necessary, ask your angel to give you a nudge whenever you even think of doing more than one task at a time.

Related to multitasking is reducing distractions. Try to quiet anything that prevents you from living in the present. If, for instance, the television is on while your partner is telling you about his or her day and makes it hard for you to concentrate, turn the television off so you can give your partner your full attention.

Smile more. When you're happy, you smile. Conversely, when you smile, you feel happy. Your facial expression tells others about your state of mind and also conveys that information to you. When you smile, you feel happy and will be able to make the most of life in the moment.

Anything involving movement encourages you to pay attention to the present moment. I gain enormous pleasure from walking, especially walking with my guardian angel. A friend of mine swims in the ocean every day of the year. Find some form of exercise that you enjoy

---

14. Leah Collins, "Job unhappiness is at a staggering all-time high, according to Gallup," *CNBC News*, August 12, 2022, https://www.cnbc.com/2022/08 /12/job-unhappiness-is-at-a-staggering-all-time-high-according-to-gallup.html.

and make it a habit. You'll benefit physically, mentally, emotionally, and spiritually.

Spend time with the people you love. We all get so involved in our everyday lives that we often fail to make time to enjoy being with good friends and family. Spending time with the people you love nourishes your soul and plays a major role in making life worth living. It's hard to worry when you're spending quality time with others, including spending time with your guardian angel.

Block out at least fifteen minutes every day to do something that you thoroughly enjoy. It might be playing a musical instrument or developing a skill, such as learning a foreign language. It could be reading a good book or browsing in a favorite store. It doesn't matter what it is, as long as it's something you can lose yourself in. While doing whatever it happens to be you'll also be practicing mindfulness, as you'll be living in the moment.

Angels of Mindfulness

All of the angels will be happy to help you eliminate fears, doubts, and worries about the past and the future, and focus on everything that's good in your life in the present moment. The main angels who focus on living in the moment are: your guardian angel, Adnachiel, Chamuel, Gabriel, Melahel, and Paschar. For Adnachiel, see chapter 12. For Chamuel, see chapter 10. For Gabriel, see chapter 7.

Melahel is one of the seventy-two Schemhamphoras, a group of angels who bear the various names of God mentioned in the Jewish scriptures. Melahel is nurturing, protective, and quick to offer consolation to people who need it. He encourages people to let go of the past and make the most of the present moment.

Paschar is an important angel who is said to be one of the seven angels who stand in front of the holy throne in heaven. He helps people who are interested in developing their psychic abilities, especially the arts of divination and prophecy. He eliminates emotional baggage and helps us visualize and manifest what we want in life.

Council of the Angels of Mindfulness

Everything you need to know about performing a Council of Angels meeting is in chapter 2. Let's assume that you want to hold a meeting to help overcome your habit of constant worrying. Make some notes ahead of time and think of the questions you'd like to ask the angels. You've decided to invite your guardian angel, Adnachiel, Chamuel, Gabriel, Melahel, and Paschar to the meeting. Everyone (including you) will need somewhere to sit, so set out seven chairs in a circle. Make sure the room is pleasantly warm and you've turned your mobile phone off.

Before the meeting, have a bath or shower and put on some clean, loose-fitting clothes.

When you're ready, sit in one of the chairs and think of some positive things that occurred during the day. Smile as you recall them. The next step is to think of your intention for the meeting. Mentally run through the questions you're planning to ask.

Take a slow, deep breath and close your eyes as you exhale. After taking a few deep breaths, visualize the room you're in filling with a beautiful golden light.

When you sense that the room is full of golden light, ask your guardian angel to invite Adnachiel, Chamuel, Gabriel, Melahel, and Paschar to the meeting. You may not hear them but will sense their presence and feel their love as they arrive, one by one.

Welcome them individually by name and smile and send love to them. Thank them for making time for you and explain exactly why you need help. You might get emotional, especially if too much worry is causing major difficulties in your life.

Once you've explained your problem in as much detail as possible, ask the angels your first question. Although your eyes are closed, you'll somehow know which angel or angels responds. Listening carefully, you notice that the angels are all respectful of each other, waiting until one angel has finished talking before having their say. You also notice that the angels appear to be of equal importance; none of them dominate the proceedings.

You ask additional questions for clarification. When all of your questions have been answered, ask if any of the angels have more advice or any suggestions they could give you. Usually they will, and sometimes they'll discuss something together before one of them tells you what they've come up with. During this stage, they may discuss topics that are not directly related to your concern. For instance, although your questions in this council meeting relate to worry, they may give you suggestions about controlling your thoughts, managing stress, and living in the present moment.

You might feel reluctant to close the meeting, as you've benefited from their advice and feel as though you've come to know the angels well. Fortunately, they agree to come back to another meeting whenever you need it.

Thank them individually, and together. Smile and wave to them as you say goodbye.

Sit quietly for a few minutes, thinking about the meeting you've just had. When you feel ready, thank the Divine for all the blessings in your life. Slowly count from one to five and open your eyes.

Have something to eat and drink, and then make notes about everything that occurred during the meeting. You'll find that your memory of the experience will be excellent, and you'll be happy with the suggestions the angels gave you.

Ritual with the Angels of Mindfulness

You can perform this ritual wherever you happen to be whenever you have a few minutes of uninterrupted time. I often perform it while sitting on a bench in a small park near my home, but I have also performed it in many other places, even in an airplane flying at 40,000 feet.

Sit down with your hands in your lap or resting on your thighs, and your feet flat on the ground. Close your eyes and become aware of your breathing. Allow your attention to focus on your heart for a several seconds, and then move on to your stomach, and down to your feet.

Become aware of your feet and the surface they're resting on. Slowly draw your attention up your legs to your buttocks and feel them resting on whatever you're sitting on. Pause and allow yourself to sense exactly how you're sitting.

When you feel ready, draw your attention up your body, into your shoulders, and down each arm to the tips of your fingers. Experience how your hands and fingers are feeling.

Allow your attention to drift up to your neck and head, and pay attention to what your eyes, nose, and ears are experiencing. With practice, you'll be able to do this ritual with your eyes open, but you'll be able to sense warmth, a slight breeze, and other sensations even with them closed. Your nose is extremely sensitive; when you focus on it, you might pick up some scents that you hadn't been aware of before. If you're outdoors, your ears will pick up birdsong, traffic noise, and other sounds. You'll even pick up a wide range of sounds that you wouldn't normally notice indoors in a quiet house.

Ask the angels of mindfulness to join you. If you wish, you might prefer to ask your guardian angel, or a specific angel of mindfulness. Ask the angel or angels to help you remain totally in the moment.

Enjoy being in the company of supportive, loving, nonjudgmental angels who are prepared to stay with you for as long as you wish.

Ask the angels if there's anything you should pay attention to. Direct your attention to whatever it happens to be, and then bring your thoughts back to the present moment.

Ask the angels for a blessing, and feel your body reacting positively as the blessing spreads to every cell of your body.

When you're ready, thank the angels of mindfulness for their help. Slowly count to five and open your eyes. Remain sitting for about a minute, and then stand up and stretch before carrying on with your day.

We've now worked with angels who'll help you love others, find your life's purpose, and become forgiving, kind, and mindful. These are all factors in leading a successful life. You won't be surprised to learn that we'll discuss the angels of encouragement who will motivate and help you achieve success in the next chapter.

Chapter Fifteen

How to Work with
the Angels of Encouragement

Everyone gets discouraged at times. It's hard to remain motivated in the face of constant problems and difficulties that seem impossible to overcome no matter how hard you work or whatever you try to accomplish. In this sort of situation, it's difficult to continue encouraging yourself until you finally succeed. Fortunately, the angels of encouragement are always ready to provide the necessary motivation, reassurance, stimulus, and help to keep you on track when you've lost your way or your goals appear impossible to achieve. After all, one of their most important tasks is to surround you with love and support.

To achieve any degree of success in life requires you to be motivated, persistent, and willing to do whatever is necessary to achieve your goals. Most people need at least some external encouragement to do this. The quickest way to do this is to ask the angels of encouragement for help.

It's hard to define success; it means different things to different people. Dictionaries define success as the achievement of an important goal. For some people, success is measured by achieving power, fame, or wealth. For others, it could be focusing on leading a worth-while life and feeling fulfilled, happy, healthy, and loved.

Arguably, the best definition of success was written by a young American woman named Bessie Anderson Stanley (1879–1952). In 1905, she entered an essay competition whose subject was "What constitutes success?" Her winning entry was published in the *Emporia Gazette* on December 11, 1905. A number of different versions of her essay have been published since then but have been frequently attributed to Ralph Waldo Emerson and Robert Louis Stevenson. Here is her winning entry:

> He has achieved success who has lived well, laughed often and loved much; who has gained the respect of intelligent men and the love of little children; who has filled his niche and accomplished his task; who has left the world better than he found it, whether by an improved poppy, a perfect poem, or a rescued soul; who has never lacked appreciation of earth's beauty or failed to express it; who has always looked for the best in others and given the best he had; whose life was an inspiration; whose memory a benediction.[15]

The angels will provide you with all the encouragement you need to achieve success but before asking them for help, decide what success means to you. Spend time thinking about what you want to be and do in this lifetime. It can be a good idea to write a list that you can keep adding to as more ideas come into your mind. Here are some possible qualities for a successful life:

---

15. "He Has Achieved Success Who Has Lived Well, Laughed Often and Loved Much," Quote Investigator website, June 26, 2012, https://quoteinvestigator .com/2012/06/26/define-success/.

A faith or philosophy of life
Helping others
A sense of gratitude
Happiness
Giving and receiving love
A close, loving relationship
Following your life's purpose
Sufficient money
Forgiving others
Children
Living in the present

Everyone is different, so your definition of success could include some, all, or none of these.

Your guardian angel is your most important angel of success. You can also call on any or all of the angels of success (Gazriel, Lauviah, Malkiel, Perpetiel, Vehuiah, and Verchiel) and encouragement (Caliel, Jophiel, Metatron, and Verchiel). (Information on Lauviah appears in chapter 11.)

Caliel is a member of the Schemhamphoras and is an angel of joy and laughter. Caliel helps people to think before acting and encourages them to be bold and aim high. He also encourages people when they're experiencing hardship and other difficulties.

Gazriel (sometimes known as Gazardiel) is often invoked to ensure the success of any enterprise. This came about because in Jewish legend, Gazriel is in charge of sunrise and sunset. Because he is actively involved in the start of every day, he can be called upon to help with any new beginnings. Gazriel is also one of the seventy angels who is invoked at childbirth, another new beginning.

Malkiel (sometimes known as Malchiel, Malkhiel, or Malquiel) is one of the three angelic princes in the Jewish Kabbalah. Malkiel provides good ideas, inspiration, and creativity. He promises success for people who are persistent, work hard, and refuse to give up when times get hard.

Perpetiel is a useful angel to invoke if you are working on a worthwhile project but are finding it difficult to accomplish. Perpetiel will encourage you to persist until you achieve success.

Vehuiah (sometimes known as Vehujah) is one of the seventy-two angels of the Jewish Schemhamphoras. Vehuiah helps people gain the confidence and self-esteem required to achieve great success.

Verchiel (sometimes known as Zerachiel) is best known for providing love, affection, and friendship. He is ruler of the zodiacal sign of Leo and according to Papus (pseudonym of the nineteenth-century French occultist Gérard Encausse), is governor of the sun. Because of the association with Leo and the sun, Verchiel is considered an angel who actively encourages people to aim high and persist until they achieve their dreams.

In addition to the angels of encouragement and success, you can also call on the four great archangels (Raphael, Michael, Gabriel, and Uriel) or any of the angels of abundance.

How to Work with the Angels of Encouragement and Success

The angels of encouragement and success are willing to help you achieve your goals but won't do anything unless you play your part. If the angels see you working diligently toward achieving a worthwhile goal, they'll be excited to work with you and will actively help to make it happen. However, they won't be quite as keen if they see you lying on a sofa thinking about all the great things you're going to accomplish but without any evidence that you're doing anything at all to make it happen.

At the very least, have a written list of all the things you need to do or be to consider yourself a success.

The following visualization can be performed with your guardian angel and the angels of success. You'll need approximately thirty minutes to perform it. With practice, you'll be able to reduce the necessary time to about twenty minutes. I almost always allow the longer time, though, as it means I can talk with the angels without feeling any pressure related to time.

Sit down in a comfortable chair, close your eyes, and take several slow, deep breaths.

Now shift your focus from your breathing to relaxing all the muscles in your body, starting with your toes and working up to the top of your head. Pay special attention to the muscles around your eyes. They are the finest muscles in your entire body; when they relax all the other muscles start to relax too.

When you feel completely relaxed, visualize yourself walking along a quiet country road. The sun is shining and you can feel a slight breeze in the air. A few fluffy clouds are floating in the sky. You can hear the sounds of birds and cattle in a nearby field. Off to one side is a hill with a path spiraling around it, leading upward to the top. For some reason, you decide to call this path "the road to success."

You stop and look at the hill. You imagine that if you climbed it, every step would bring you closer to your goals. You smile as you wonder if you should take the road to success. At that moment, your mind tells you yes, and you know that your guardian angel is putting thoughts into your head. "Please join me," you say, and instantly you feel your guardian angel walking beside you.

Together you climb over a wooden fence, and walk across a field to the base of the hill. As you take the first steps on the path, your guardian angel asks, "Tell me, what does success mean to you?" You feel relieved that you've spent time creating a list of everything you felt necessary for success in your terms and are able to give a concise yet detailed reply.

Your guardian angel smiles and nods as you talk. "That's good. I think this is a good time to introduce you to some of my friends." Your guardian angel waves a hand, and immediately an angel appears in front of you. "Meet my friend, Vehuiah." Vehuiah has a friendly smile and a musical voice. "I'm here to fill you with the confidence and self-belief you'll need to achieve your goals. Are you ready to receive what I have to offer?" "Yes, please," you reply. Vehuiah steps forward and you find yourself enveloped in a huge hug. You feel a surge of confidence in every fiber of your being. Vehuiah steps back and says, "That should be enough for now. Remember to call on me whenever you need help." You barely have time to say thank you before Vehuiah disappears. Your guardian angel smiles, and says, "Let's keep on climbing."

You and your guardian angel start walking again. After several minutes, your guardian angel stops and waves his hand. This time you aren't surprised when another angel appears. "This is my friend, Gazriel." Gazriel extends a hand, and you feel a volt of energy as you shake it. "I'm here to help you get started," Gazriel says. "Once you've completed your plans, I'll look over them and make sure you're heading in the right direction. Please call on me whenever you need help or advice. I'm always here for you." After you've said thank you, Gazriel fades from sight.

You and your guardian angel start walking again. As you near the summit, the road gets steeper. After a few minutes, your guardian angel stops and again waves a hand. Immediately, another angel appears. "I am Verchiel," the angel says. "I'm going to help you stay motivated even when times are hard, and I'll continue encouraging and helping you until you've achieved your goals. You possess all the qualities necessary to achieve success. Aim high and fulfill your dreams." Verchiel places a hand on top of your head, and you experience a surge of positive energy in every cell of your body. Verchiel smiles at you and vanishes from view.

Your guardian angel takes you by the hand, and together you walk to the top of the hill. "Look around," your guardian angel says. "You have unlimited potential, and everything you can see is attainable. Are you prepared to do whatever is necessary to achieve your goals?" When you confirm that you are, your guardian angel says, "Believe in yourself." Together you run back down the hill, laughing all the way. When you reach the country road again, your guardian angel hugs you, says goodbye, and fades away. You find yourself back in your comfortable chair. Think about your visualization for a minute or two before silently counting from one to five and opening your eyes.

You can repeat this visualization as often as you wish. It's a good idea to change the angels you speak to every now and again. You should also include any angels who have a special interest in the areas you want to achieve success in (see the appendix).

The final type of angels we're going to meet are the angels of abundance. Abundance means having enough of something to satisfy your immediate needs. An abundance of money is, of course, a good thing, but the angels of abundance are interested in much more than that. In the next chapter you'll find that the angels of abundance want you to enjoy a life that is abundant in every way. Success is not always measured in monetary terms, although money does have an important part to play in everyone's life. There are specific angels of money who are willing to help you manage your financial affairs. We'll meet them in the next chapter.

Chapter Sixteen

How to Work with the Angels of Abundance

I find it interesting that whenever I say the word "abundance," people tend to think of it solely in terms of money. This isn't surprising, as the word actually means having a plentiful supply, or an ample amount, of something: an abundance of sunshine, an abundance of friends, an abundance of opportunities, an abundance of time, or an abundant garden. Someone who leads an abundant life experiences great joy and happiness, and also enjoys good health, enriching friendships, and a close connection between their body, mind, and soul. This person would have a positive mindset, be generous, kind, and forgiving, and see the best in everyone they encountered. They could be rich or poor financially but would enjoy a full and rich life regardless.

Possibly the best definition of abundance I've heard was told to me by a friend. "It's a feeling of freedom. I can order a meal at a restaurant without worrying about having enough money on my card to pay for it. It's being able to spend time with the favorite people in my life. It's looking after myself physically and mentally, so I keep fit and well. Most of all, it's a sense of security that no matter what happens, I'll always be able to get the maximum enjoyment out of life."

The good news is that you can enjoy an abundance of whatever it is you want, and the angels of abundance are more than willing to help you achieve it.

Angels of Abundance

A number of angels have a special interest in helping people gain abundance in their lives. They include your guardian angel, Barbelo, Barchiel, Cahatel, Gadiel, Gamaliel, Isda, Pathiel, and Raziel. These angels can help you overcome problems such as a scarcity mindset and negative thoughts about what you can and can't have in life. They can work behind the scenes to provide you with opportunities to progress in life and ultimately enjoy a life full of abundance. Cahatel's information appears in chapter 7. Raziel's information is in chapter 15.

Your guardian angel is your most important angel of success and will do everything possible to help you achieve your goals. However, you need to let your angel know exactly what it is that you want to achieve. It's hard for your angel to help without knowing what your goal is.

Barbelo is a female archon and an angel of abundance and prosperity. Archons are a high-ranking order of angels in the Gnostic tradition who have the responsibility of looking after countries and large groups of people. The four main archangels (Raphael, Michael, Gabriel, and Uriel) are said to be members of the archons. Although angels are normally considered to be genderless, Barbelo has always been described as female. You can call on Barbelo whenever you need good luck, prosperity, and abundance. Make sure to thank Barbelo once you achieve these things, as, if you forget or neglect to do it, your good fortune will disappear.

Barchiel ("God's blessings") has always been considered an important angel and is often thought to be one of the seven traditional archangels. He is responsible for people born under the signs of Scorpio and Pisces. Barchiel helps people maintain a positive outlook on life and provides sound financial advice and good fortune. He'll keep you firmly focused on your goals of achieving abundance in every area of your life.

Gadiel ("God is my wealth") is one of the most revered angels in heaven and is said to protect people against evil. He'll provide you with opportunities to slowly but steadily improve your financial situation, achieve abundance, and gain status in the community.

In the Gnostic writings and the Kabbalah, Gamaliel (which means "Recompense of God") is considered a kind-hearted, benevolent angel. He carries blessings of money, joy, happiness, and good luck from God to people who deserve them. He's extremely generous to people who have done good deeds. Because he hands out rewards so frequently, he's considered one of the most bountiful and magnanimous of the angels of abundance.

Raziel's name means "Secret of God." He's an important angel who's willing to use his knowledge of the universe to help you achieve success. He's said to be a member of the Sarim, the angel princes in heaven. He's also a prince of the order of Thrones and a member of the cherubim. He has many other titles, including Angel of Originality and Angel of Supreme Mysteries. Raziel enjoys helping original thinkers develop their ideas and achieve success. He also enjoys answering imponderable questions. Raziel is a wise angel who has a special interest in magic and knowledge. He helps people realize that their possibilities are limitless, and they can and should aim high. Once they've done that, Raziel will provide advice until they've achieved their goals.

According to Jewish legend, Raziel felt sorry for Adam and Eve when they were banished from the Garden of Eden, and gave Adam the Book of the Angel Raziel. This book contained all the knowledge of the universe and enabled the couple to make a life for themselves outside the garden. This same book later enabled Enoch to become the wisest man of his time and provided Noah with all the information he needed to build his ark. Hundreds of years later, the book was owned by King Solomon, who used it to create magic. After his death, the book disappeared. Unfortunately, this is simply a story; the actual *Book of the Angel Raziel* was written in medieval times, probably by Eleazor of Worms (ca. 1160–1237).

Isda may seem an unlikely angel of abundance; she is concerned with physical, emotional, and spiritual nourishment. Due to her interest in physical nourishment, she is sometimes known as the angel of food. Because she provides as much good-quality food as required, she has over the years become associated with abundance.

Thousands of years ago, Jewish mystics invoked Pathiel ("the opener") at the end of Sabbath, confident that he would provide them with wealth and abundance. People still invoke him for the same reasons today. Pathiel enjoys surprising people; if you ask him for help, he'll present you with a variety of opportunities for abundance and success. He's likely to give you unexpected blessings that will provide you with increased happiness as well as abundance.

Limiting Beliefs

Before starting to work on abundance, it's important to eliminate any limiting beliefs you may have, the false stories we tell ourselves that hold us back from becoming the magnificent, glorious people full of latent potential that we actually are. It's especially sad that many of these are subconscious beliefs that we're unaware of until someone tells us about them.

Limiting beliefs often begin in childhood when we accept something someone said as being the truth. When I was in high school, my French teacher told me that I was useless at languages, something I believed for more than thirty years. The first time I went to the Frankfurt Book Fair in Germany, I had to buy all my meals at McDonald's, where I was able to point at the menu to indicate what I wanted. When I attended the book fair the following year, I was able to eat anywhere, as I'd discovered that I was actually good at learning languages and it was exciting to be able to talk to people in another language. I'd accepted what my French teacher told me because he was an authority figure, and it had never occurred to me that he was wrong.

Similarly, I heard my mother sing only once. She was told by a teacher at school that she couldn't sing, so she only did so when she was certain no one could hear her. She actually sang well, but telling her that didn't work; the ingrained limiting belief was too strong.

A limiting belief doesn't necessarily involve someone telling you that you aren't good at something, either. Have you ever said to yourself, "I'm no good at [whatever it happens to be], so why even try?" We can all be our own worst enemy in many ways.

Common examples of limiting beliefs include thinking you are too old (or too young) to do or be something, feeling as though you aren't good enough, thinking you don't have enough money, thinking you'll never be successful, believing that you aren't intelligent enough, or that you don't deserve love. Your brain creates these beliefs when trying to protect you from hurt and pain in the future. Fortunately, you can eliminate these blocks and start leading a life full of abundance.

The first step is to identify the limiting beliefs that prevent you from living the life you deserve. All you need do is sit quietly with pen and paper and write down everything that you're afraid of. When you first do this exercise, you'll probably be surprised at the number of subconscious and conscious fears that you have. It doesn't matter how many you identify; with the help of Metatron and Raziel, you'll eliminate them all, one at a time.

Next, choose one limiting belief and write down five reasons why you're afraid of whatever it happens to be. For instance, if you listed "I don't deserve love," your five reasons why you're afraid might be: "I'm not attractive or interesting enough," "I'm not a good person," "My marriage ended after two years, and I've found it hard to commit to anyone else since then," "I found it hard to trust anyone after I was betrayed when I was seventeen," and "When I went on a blind date, it ended after only five minutes."

Once you have your five reasons, you need to disprove them all. Try to come up with five reasons why each of these statements is wrong. If you wrote about it being hard to commit after a painful divorce, you might write: "We were both far too young and immature to get married, but I'm older and wiser now. My expectations were unrealistic and I blamed my partner for everything that went wrong. I now realize that I wasn't being fair and that we were both to blame. I knew nothing about money, and the endless arguments we had about our finances ultimately destroyed our relationship. I'm better with money now, and am able to live within my income. I lacked trust and was suspicious whenever my partner was away for too long. It's taken me a while, but I've learned the lesson of trust. I bottled up my feelings too much—whenever I exploded, I was hard, cruel, and unfair. I've learned how to handle my feelings, and am able to deal with them much better now."

Finally, write down a new belief. To continue the example earlier: "I have learned from experience and am older and wiser now. I know that I can find and keep a good, strong, loving relationship with the right person. When the time is right, I'll be able to commit totally to the relationship."

You can make the experience much more effective by asking the great angel Metatron to guide you through the process. Metatron will encourage you to repeat the exercise as frequently as you can until the false belief has been completely replaced by the new, true belief.

Eliminating Negative Beliefs Visualization with Metatron

Start by sitting down somewhere where you won't be disturbed for at least thirty minutes. Wear warm, loose-fitting clothes. Relax all the muscles in your body using any of the methods covered earlier.

When you feel fully relaxed, start talking to your guardian angel about your limiting beliefs and how you've decided to eliminate them from your life. Ask your guardian angel to contact the great angel Metatron and ask for help to eliminate them.

Sit quietly and think about the limiting belief you most want to eliminate. After a minute or two, you'll sense that Metatron is with you. You'll feel his incredible strength, love, and compassion surrounding and enfolding you in a loving embrace. Thank him for coming to your aid and tell him about the limiting belief that's holding you back. Tell him the five reasons you came up with that make you feel afraid, and wait for his response.

Metatron's answer will come in a number of ways. You might be fortunate enough to hear his voice, but the response is more likely to come as thoughts in your mind along with a deep sense of peace. You might feel him holding you close or simply gain a sense that the problem no longer exists. He may go through the five reasons you thought of that show this limiting belief is false and tell you that you can let it go. You may or may not feel it necessary to tell Metatron your new positive belief. If you feel that the old belief has completely vanished, you may choose to simply relax and enjoy basking in Metatron's love.

Metatron is patient and will stay with you for as long as you wish. When you feel the time is right, thank him and spend a minute or two thinking about what you learned. Next, thank your guardian angel for arranging the meeting.

Finally, count slowly from one to five, confident that the matter has been completely resolved.

Once the matter has been resolved, you won't need to do anything more about that particular old belief and can call on Metatron to help you with the next self-limiting belief you have on your list. If you have any doubts at all about the first self-limiting belief, ask your guardian angel to arrange another meeting with Metatron. It's common to need more than one meeting because self-limiting beliefs become deeply entrenched in the psyche; it can take several rituals to eliminate them permanently. Metatron will be only too pleased to guide you through this ritual as many times as necessary to eliminate the problem.

Manifestation

Manifestation means making your dreams come true. You can manifest or attain anything you want. To be successful, you need to know what you want, believe it's possible, ask the angels to help you, be prepared to do whatever work is necessary, nurture your goal with enthusiasm and energy, and remain fixed on whatever it is you want to manifest until you have it in your life. In addition to manifesting abundance, you can also manifest states of mind such as confidence, self-esteem, personal security, and inner peace. Manifestations of this sort can completely change your life.

Countless millions of people in the world have no idea what they want in life. I read somewhere that most people put more thought and effort into planning a summer vacation than they do into planning their lives. These people are like ships without a rudder. The first and most important step to leading an abundant life is to know what you want.

If you haven't yet discovered what you want out of this lifetime, think about the things that you're passionate about. Everyone is passionate about something. Do you get excited about music, cooking, basketball, stamp collecting, playing the guitar, or helping others? Think about the things you get excited about and examine them to see if you can find your life purpose there. Once you decide what you want, the universe will start working on your behalf to enable you to achieve it.

Have you ever become lost in doing something and were amazed at how many hours had passed by while you were in the flow? That could be a major clue about your passion.

Your guardian angel knows you better than anyone. Ask your angel for suggestions and advice on what you should be doing in this incarnation.

Most of what we've covered so far relates to your purpose in life. Right now, you might simply want to replace your car with something newer and better—that's a worthwhile goal! You might want to find a better job with more responsibility and pay. You might want to buy a new computer or even a house. All of these things relate to abundance, and you should ask the universe to satisfy your material desires because you are as worthy as anyone else. Be as specific as possible with whatever it is you wish to manifest. Don't ask for "a new car"; specify the model, the color, and features you want it to have.

If you intend to ask for money, be careful: money is important, but you'll achieve better results by asking directly for what you want rather than enough money to be able to purchase it. The exception to this is when you need a specific amount of money to be applied to a number of different purposes. Let's assume you want $10,000 in the next six weeks to pay off your credit cards, book a vacation, and take a prospective partner to dinner at an expensive restaurant. As long as you know exactly where the money is going, this is a good way to combine several intentions.

In addition to achieving abundance materially, you should also set abundance goals for other areas of your life. Physical abundance means looking after your body and enjoying radiant health and vitality. Mental abundance involves keeping mentally stimulated and learning new things all the way through life. Emotional abundance means enjoying deep, fulfilling relationships with yourself and others. Spiritual abundance means developing a close connection with the Divine.

The intent or intention is your goal, which is whatever it is you want to manifest in your life. Intention is the driving force that provides you with the necessary energy and motivation to achieve your goal. Once you've set your intent, you need to trust and believe in it until it manifests and becomes part of your life. Most people daydream about what they want and how they'd like their lives to be, but few people set their mind on an important goal—their intent—and make it happen.

This is because people constantly change their minds. They may want something now but then want something completely different a few days later. Wishful thinking is fun, but these thoughts become an intent only when you make up your mind that what you've been daydreaming about is something you really want to achieve.

Your intentions can be big or small, and there's no reason why you can't do both. I tell people who are skeptical about the process to set a small intention for themselves and to then aim for something larger once they've seen that it works. Fortunately, small intentions usually manifest quickly. A year or two ago, a friend told me how she manifested a book. I thought that was a great idea and told the universe that I wanted to receive a book within three days. I didn't specify a particular book, as it was purely an exercise in manifestation. Two days later, a courier driver handed me a small packet containing a book written by a friend—I had no idea that he'd written one! I was excited to receive the book and told many people about my exercise in manifestation. Several people told me I would have received the book anyway, which is true. However, it was sent from Washington, D.C., and took just three days to reach me in New Zealand. Maybe the universe sped everything up to ensure that I received it within my three-day deadline.

You can ask the angels of abundance to help you set a suitable intention for yourself. It's a good idea to perform this ritual even if you think you know what you want because you (and every other person on the planet) constantly send out a variety of often conflicting intents created by your thoughts and actions every day. Everyone does this, usually unconsciously so we aren't aware of it. This process works well when you attract good things into your life but can just as easily work against you and attract what you don't want because negative thoughts and feelings produce negative results. The angels will help you create an intention that is right for you.

Before starting this ritual, ask yourself questions to help formulate a suitable intention. You might ask:

- What is the most important thing in my life?
- What would I like more of in this lifetime?
- What would I like to eliminate, or let go of?
- What would I like my legacy to be?
- What makes me feel proud?
- What am I grateful for?
- What holds me back from achieving my dreams?

Your answers will provide you with ideas about what intention may be right for you.

Angel Intention Council Meeting

Start by relaxing in your usual way.

Once you're fully relaxed, ask your guardian angel to invite Archangel Michael and the angels of abundance to join you. If you wish, you can also specify specific angels. You'll become aware of their presence almost as soon as you make your request.

Thank them for coming to help you and tell them that you want more abundance in your life, along with the ability to choose something that aligns with your beliefs and values. Your beliefs are ideas and concepts that you believe to be true and are not necessarily related to organized religion. Values are ideas that you consider to be vitally important and determine how you interact and deal with others. Together, beliefs and values represent our attitudes and ideas. To be successful, your intention must relate to your beliefs and values.

Tell the angels about your intentions, and ask for advice on whether or not they are worthy goals for you and if they harmonize with your beliefs and values.

Sit quietly and wait for their responses. You'll probably receive their replies as thoughts, though it's possible you'll hear them as voices close to your ear. The angels may agree with what you've come up with, suggest changing some of your ideas, or they may suggest something else entirely. If your intention is to own a multi-million-dollar home but the angels suggest that you focus on giving and receiving love, you'll have a great deal to discuss.

Ask questions and listen to the answers. You may ask a specific angel to answer a question or two, but usually it's better to invite all of them to respond. By the end of the session, you may or may not have decided on a suitable intention. Either way, you'll have plenty to think about. You can repeat this ritual regularly until you find a suitable intention that works with your beliefs and values and has the approval of the angels of abundance.

Thank Archangel Michael and the angels of abundance for their insights, help, and encouragement.

Sit quietly for a minute or two, and then count silently from one to five, and open your eyes.

Affirmations

Once you've decided on a specific intention, create an affirmation, which is a short positive sentence that thanks the Divine for giving you whatever your goal happens to be. This sentence should be written in the present tense, as if you've already achieved the result you desire.

Here's an example. Let's assume you've been suffering from self-doubt and low self-esteem and want to manifest happiness and confidence. A suitable affirmation might be: "I feel good about myself and experience joy and positivity everywhere I go."

Once you've written your affirmation, repeat it as often as you can, silently and out loud. This impresses your intention on your subconscious mind and helps make it a reality in your life. Whenever you have a spare moment during the day, repeat your affirmations to yourself. Whenever you have a spare moment, such as when you're waiting, can be put to good, constructive use by repeating your affirmations. Another good time to say them is while waiting for sleep, as they help you experience positive and productive dreams that relate to your intentions. Whenever you find yourself thinking negative thoughts, eliminate them by silently saying your affirmations.

Angelic Success Ritual

You need to constantly feed your goal with positivity and energy. Say your affirmations with enthusiasm. You must visualize your intention as if you've already achieved it, and imagine scenarios in which you're enjoying all the joys that the manifestation has brought into your life. It's important to start by visualizing the successful conclusion of your goal, which enables you to experience the feelings of fulfillment and satisfaction you'll have when you achieve it. These feelings effect change on a subtle level and change your future to include your intention.

You should not perform the Angelic Success Ritual until after you've visualized a scene in which you're appreciating or celebrating the successful outcome of your intention and repeated it several times. I like to sit down in a comfortable chair, close my eyes, and think about different ways I could celebrate a successful outcome. Once I've decided exactly how I'll picture it in my mind, I perform it every night in bed before falling asleep. I fall asleep quickly after going through this visualization, and I'm sure doing it immediately before falling asleep ensures that my subconscious mind will work on it while I'm sleeping.

You can do this visualization for any intention. You'll need approximately thirty minutes of uninterrupted time. Wear loose-fitting clothes, and make sure that the room is reasonably warm.

Sit down in a comfortable chair, close your eyes, and relax.

Start talking to your guardian angel about what's been going on in your life. Once you've brought your angel up to date with your news, ask any questions you might have and then ask if the angels of abundance could join you; you want to thank them for helping you to manifest (whatever it happens to be). You can call on specific angels of abundance if you prefer.

Once you sense their presence, thank them sincerely for their help and tell them that you'd like to show them the visualization you've created to celebrate the manifestation of your intention. You might hear some comments or replies, and you'll probably sense that you're now encircled by the angels of abundance. You'll experience a great feeling of comfort and love.

When you're ready, go through the visualization in your mind. When you've finished, see yourself in your mind's eye turning in a circle and thanking all the angels for their help and support as well as enabling you to achieve your intention.

Sense your guardian angel standing beside you as you turn around again. "Thank you, my friend," you say. "Not only for arranging this but also for everything you do for me."

Speak with the angels of abundance and ask them if you should modify your visualization in any way. Listen to what they may have to say. When they've finished, express your gratitude to them for all the work they do. Say goodbye to them one by one as they leave. Once they've left, thank your guardian angel for asking the angels of abundance to join you.

"They'll be working for you behind the scenes, to help you achieve this goal," your guardian angel says. "And I'm always here to help you, too." Your guardian angel gives you a hug and then disappears.

Spend a minute or two thinking about what you've accomplished. When you feel ready, count slowly from one to five, and open your eyes.

There's no need to repeat this ritual, but you should continue to perform your visualization as often as you can until it manifests in your life.

Money

Success is not necessarily measured in monetary terms, but money nevertheless has an important part to play in everyone's life. Everyone knows the old saying that says money doesn't buy happiness. Researchers have found that as long as you're making enough money to make ends meet, money has little or no long-term effect on happiness. A significant pay raise makes people happier for a short period of time, but they soon return to their former state of happiness. In their 2010 article "High income improves evaluation of life but not emotional well-being," Dr. Daniel Kahneman and Sir Angus Deaton of Princeton University wrote that when people were asked what made them happy yesterday, they mentioned family and friends, working on a project with others, and other similar replies but didn't mention money. Yet when they were asked what would make them happier, the most common reply was "more money."[16] And although money on its own doesn't buy happiness, sufficient money acts as a safety net and makes life easier. Unfortunately, many people today struggle to make ends meet, which causes a great deal of stress, worry, and sleepless nights.

Angels of Money

Fortuitously, there are many angels who specialize in helping people handle financial blocks and other problems. These include Ariel, Asmodel, Barchiel, Haniel, Jeremiel, Raziel, Sachiel, Uriel, and Zadkiel. For information on Uriel, see chapter 7. For information on Zadkiel, see chapter 12. Information on Raziel appears earlier in this chapter.

Ariel is one of the ruling angels of the zodiac and is responsible for the sign of Leo. He's also a member of the Schemhamphoras. Ariel is an extremely positive and enthusiastic angel who enjoys helping people set goals and achieve their ambitions. Ariel provides guidance and advice for people at any stage of their careers.

Asmodel is responsible for people born under the sign of Taurus. He can be called upon for any financial matters. He is cautious

---

16. Daniel Kahneman and Angus Deaton, "High income improves evaluation of life but not emotional well-being," *Proceedings of the National Academy of Science* vol. 107, no. 38, August 4, 2010, https://www.pnas.org/doi/10.1073/pnas.1011492107.

and helps people to slowly but steadily increase their net worth. He encourages people to be patient and avoid get-rich-quick schemes.

Haniel's name means "Glory of God." He is a planetary angel and is one of the rulers of the planet Venus. Haniel will reignite your zest for life, encourage a positive mindset, and give you the necessary ambition and drive to achieve your financial goals.

The name Jeremiel means "God's Mercy." Archangel Jeremiel is an angel of mercy and forgiveness. He enjoys helping people who are at a crossroads in their lives, and are not sure which is the best path for them. He is known as the angel of visions and dreams, and frequently gives advice to people while they're dreaming. Jeremiel provides sound financial advice, by carefully evaluating the long-term effects of different choices. (You can find more information about Archangel Jeremiel in chapter 12.)

The name Sachiel means "Covering of God." Sachiel is considered the archangel of Jupiter, the planet of expansion and growth. He is also interested in legal matters, good fortune, wealth, success, and generosity. Sachiel is willing to help people earn money and progress financially, but will not help anyone obtain money for nothing.

How to Eliminate Negative Thoughts about Money

We start learning about money from an early age, usually from our parents. Unfortunately, much of what we learn can have long-term implications and hold us back financially. If you grew up hearing and now believe that "money doesn't grow on trees," you've accepted one of the most common limiting beliefs about money. Your parents were effectively telling you that money has to be earned and, as a limited resource, must be spent carefully. There are many other limiting beliefs that you might have accepted, such as: "There's not enough money to go around," "I don't deserve a lot of money," "Having money is selfish," "You need money to make money," "Money can't buy happiness," "Money is the root of all evil," "I'm not good with money," and "My family has always been poor." If you've accepted any of these as being true, you'll remain short of money until you eliminate this negative belief.

Fortunately, Archangel Jeremiel will help you eliminate all the negative thoughts you may have about money.

Feelings about Money

Make a list of all the feelings you have about money, both positive and negative. If you're like most people, you'll have more negative than positive feelings on your list.

Read each item one at a time, and see what feelings you experience in your body. You may feel a tightening in your stomach or chest, you could feel angry or ill, or even a sense of dread. Everyone's different, but pay special attention to the ones that have most effect on you. If any of the items on your list promote a strong response, you should perform the ritual below purely for them. If your body gives you the same reaction to all of the items, you can include all of them in the ritual.

Feelings about Money Ritual with Jeremiel

You can perform the following ritual as often as you wish. You should notice an improvement in your feelings about money right away, but repetition will speed up the process of completely changing your mindset.

You can also perform this ritual (or an abbreviated form of it) wherever you happen to be. Many years ago, I did this while waiting in line at my local bank. It seemed to be an appropriate place to do it, and I had enough time to perform most of it.

Start by creating your sacred space and gaining protection by performing the Angelic Invocation of Protection in chapter 2.

Stand or sit in the center of your circle facing east. Close your eyes, and ask your guardian angel to stay close beside you while you perform the ritual. Ask your angel to invite Archangel Jeremiel to join you.

While you're waiting for Jeremiel to appear, visualize yourself walking along a quiet country road. It's dusk, and as you walk, you ask yourself why you've always had such negative thoughts and feelings about money. Ahead you see a sign indicating four directions. A minute later you find yourself at a crossroads. It seems appropriate, as you know that Jeremiel helps people who are at a crossroads in their life. You stop walking and look in all four directions. All the roads are deserted, and it seems as if you have the whole world to yourself. You turn around again, and find you've been joined by a tall, good-looking man wearing purple robes. He has an aura of peace surrounding him, and you can see his love and sense of humor in his eyes. "Hello," he says. "I'm Jeremiel." He has a deep, sonorous voice.

You find it hard to speak for a few moments but introduce yourself, and thank him for coming to your aid. He rests a hand on your shoulder and asks you to tell him all about your concerns with money. He gazes deeply into your eyes as you tell him about your experiences with money over the years. You even surprise yourself with some long-forgotten memories about money when you were young. When you've finished, you tell him that you want to eliminate all your negative feelings about money and want to start moving forward financially.

When you've finished, Jeremiel nods his head a few times. He asks, "Could I read the notes you wrote down, please?" You find the piece of paper you wrote your thoughts about money on, and hand it to Jeremiel. He reads it slowly. "Let's have a life review," he says, "to make sure I've absorbed everything you've told me." Instantly, you see yourself as a small child reenacting everything that happened in your first experience with money. The visualization is perfect: you can clearly see the scene in your mind, and everyone in it looks exactly the same as they did at the time of your experience. Next, you move on to another scene where you gained negative feelings about money. This process continues rapidly, scene after scene, until you're back in the present moment. Jeremiel asks if the visualization included everything you could remember about money. You respond affirmatively.

"I understand what's happened," Jeremiel says. "Firstly, you need to forgive yourself for picking up these negative feelings. It's not your fault, as what you did is perfectly natural under the circumstances. However, you still need to forgive yourself, and everyone else who deliberately or unintentionally gave you these mistaken beliefs. Can you do that? Are you willing to forgive yourself and others?" "Yes," you reply in a strong voice.

"Good," Jeremiel says. "Take a deep breath, and exhale slowly." You do as he says, and suddenly the environment you're in starts circling around you, slowly at first, but gradually gathering speed until all you can see are flashes of light speeding around you. "Don't be afraid," Jeremiel says. "I'm with you. Right now, I want you to let go of all those negative experiences. Release them from your heart, mind, and body, and let them disappear into the vortex surrounding you." Several seconds later, Jeremiel says, "Say out loud that you're forgiving yourself." "I forgive myself," you say. "Good, and now forgive everyone else." "I forgive everyone who has ever given me negative feelings about money."

As soon as you stop speaking, the vortex surrounding you slows down and stops. You find yourself back at the crossroads with Jeremiel and your guardian angel. Something looks different, though, and you laugh as you suddenly see the world has changed into a glorious, positive place. All the colors are vibrant, and everything looks brand new. Jeremiel gives you time to realize that you're in a brand-new world, and then says, "Now it's time to fill you with positive thoughts about money." Your environment starts circling around you again, faster and faster. You can hear Jeremiel instilling positive thoughts into your heart, mind, and body. "I respect money. I'm worthy of the best life has to offer. People with money aren't bad. Money is neither good nor bad. Money is neutral. I set financial goals. I recognize opportunities, and make plans to achieve my financial goals. I am grateful for everything I'm learning about money." You can sense Jeremiel's words reaching every cell of your body, and feel your body accepting them. You stop paying attention to the words, as you know they're all good for you. After what seems like only a second or two, the vortex slows down and you're back in your world made new. You realize your smile is wider than it's ever been before. You feel free of all past financial limitations, and you can hardly wait to start moving forward financially. You look up at Jeremiel's smiling face and thank him sincerely. He replies that he's happy to help you whenever you need it, and says goodbye. As soon as you've responded with a good-bye, Jeremiel disappears from view, leaving you and your guardian angel standing at the crossroads.

You ask your guardian angel to tell you which road to take. Your angel indicates the road in front of you. "Let's walk the road to success," you say. You and your guardian angel laugh as you start walking. You feel freer, happier, and more in control than you've ever felt before. It takes no time for you to arrive back at your sacred space. Once you've become familiar with the situation you're in, close the circle by thanking and dismissing the four archangels. When you feel ready, count to five, open your eyes, and carry on with your day.

Conclusion

Developing a closer connection with the angels will automatically bring you closer to the Divine, and you'll experience universal consciousness, the awareness that you're an intrinsic part of the web of life. This oneness of being will provide you with a sense of joy and incredible peace as well as the knowledge that you are connected with all of creation and your life is important. Nothing will ever hold you back because you know that you can achieve anything you wish. You'll know that you don't have to be perfect; all you need to do is the very best that you can.

When people reach the end of their lives, they have no regrets about their possessions or investments. They aren't concerned about missed promotions or that their neighbor drove a better car than they did. Most people regret the things they didn't say or do, as well as the opportunities they failed to seize. They regret not telling the special people in their lives how much they loved them and wish they'd hugged them more often than they did.

Your angels will help you reach the end of your life with few regrets, as you'll have accomplished all you need to do in this incarnation. Contact your angels every day. Tell them what you want and need, and let them help you achieve your spiritual and self-improvement goals.

Appendix

The visualizations and rituals in this book can be adapted and used for other purposes beyond what was covered in detail. Here's a comprehensive list of angels that you can work with for almost every need.

Abundance (*See* Manifestation *and* Wealth): Aladiah, Ariel, Barbelo, Barchiel, Cahatel, Gadiel, Gamaliel, Isda, Lecabel, Mebahel, Omael, Pathiel, Raphael, Raziel, Zadkiel

Acceptance: Anael, Chamuel, Isda, Uzziel, Zaphkiel

Achievement: Raphael

Adaptability: Haaiah, Melahel, Raphael

Addictions (overcoming): Adnachiel, Aniel, Baglis, Barbelo, Gabriel, Hariel, Ieiazel, Metatron, Michael, Raphael, Uriel

Adversity (to overcome): Caliel, Jeremiel, Leuviah, Michael, Sitael

Agriculture: Omael

Akashic Records (accessing): Metatron

Alchemy: Raziel, Uriel

Alcoholism: Raphael, Uriel

Altruism: Lauviah, Mebahel, Yehuiah

Anger (controlling): Affafniel, Amitiel, Balthiel, Hemah, Qispiel, Raguel, Raphael, Uriel

Animals (protecting and healing): Afriel, Ariel, Asariel (especially horses), Behemiel, Hariel, Jehiel, Nemamiah, Orifiel, Sandalphon

Anxiety: Adnachiel, Rehael, Uriel

Appreciation: Ieiazel, Yehuiah

Arts (success in): Akriel, Haamiah, Gabriel, Hael, Hariel, Ieiazel, Jophiel, Lelahel

Assertiveness: Bath Kol

Astrology: Barbiel

Authority: Elemiah, Gabriel, Rehael

Balance (work/life): Caliel

Beauty: Haamiah, Hael, Jophiel, Uriel

Benevolence: Hasdiel, Vasariah

Bereavement: Yehudiah

Birds (protection of): Anpiel, Ariel, Orifiel, Sandalphon

Blessings (to send): Amitiel, Barchiel, Cahetel, Gabriel, Hael, Sandalphon

Blockages (removing): Lahabiel, Michael

Business (success in): Anael, Asmodel, Ieiaiel, Mihr, Yeiayel

Career: Ambriel, Asmodel, Chamuel, Jeremiel

Caring (for others): Haamiah

Ceremonies: Haamiah

Chakras: Caliel, Chamuel, Gabriel, Jophiel, Michael, Raphael, Uriel, Zadkiel

Change: Caliel, Metatron, Raziel

Childbirth: Amariel, Armisael, Gabriel, Isda, Laylah, Rachmiel, Sandalphon, Temeluch, Zuriel

Children: Adnachiel, Diniel, Gabriel, Metatron, Michael, Nemamiah, Raphael, Sandalphon, Temeluch, Zaphkiel, Zuriel

Clairvoyance: Asariel, Azrael, Gabriel, Hanael, Jeremiel, Michael, Raphael, Raziel

Clarity: Amitiel, Jeremiel, Jophiel, Uriel

Cleanliness: Hahaiah

Cleansing: Lahabiel

Clearing: Gabriel

Commitment: Caliel, Isda, Mebahel, Yehuiah

Communication: Ambriel, Bath Kol, Gabriel, Iezalel, Raphael, Sariel, Zachariel

Compassion: Balthiel, Chamuel, Hanael, Lahabiel, Rahmiel, Raphael, Sariel, Sophia, Tiphareth, Vasariah, Zadkiel, Zaphkiel

Concentration: Nelkhael, Vehuiah

Conception: Armisael, Cahetel, Gabriel, Lailah, Zuriel

Confidence: Adnachiel, Anael, Barchiel, Ihiazel, Jehudiel, Lahabiel, Lauviah, Metatron, Michael, Reiyel, Vehujah, Yerathel

Conflict: Chamuel

Confusion: Adnachiel, Amitiel, Metatron

Conscience: Caliel

Consolation: Ieiazel

Contemplation: Cassiel

Contentment: Uzziel

Contracts: Michael

Cooperation: Raguel

Courage: Adnachiel, Camael, Chamuel, Iahel, Machidael, Metatron, Michael, Pahaliah, Raphael, Samael, Uriel

Creativity: Adnachiel, Anael, Asariel, Bath Kol, Chamuel, Gabriel, Ieiazel, Jophiel, Lelahel, Liwet, Mizrael, Raphael, Raziel, Teiazel, Uriel, Vehael

Criticism (accepting): Chamuel

Death *(See also* **Reincarnation** *and* **Transition):** Azrael, Cassiel, Gabriel, Kafziel, Metatron, Michael, Suriel, Yehudiah

Death of an animal: Meshabber

Deception: Amitiel, Gabriel

Decision making: Lecabel

Dedication: Menadel

Depression (overcoming): Azrael, Bath Kol, Isda, Metatron, Raziel, Rehael, Remiel

Detachment: Melchizedek

Devotion: Lauviah, Lehahiah

Difficulties, overcoming: Sitael

Diplomacy: Yeiayel

Discernment: Raziel

Discipline: Lehahiah

Discretion: Haaiah

Divination *(See* **Intuition):** Adad, Asariel, Gabriel, Isaiel, Paschar, Teiaiel

Divorce: Bethnael, Gabriel, Michael, Pallas, Raphael, Uriel

Domestic violence (to stop): Michael, Uriel

Domestic violence (healing): Gabriel

Dreams (to encourage): Adnachiel, Duma, Gabriel, Jeremiel, Mahasiah, Raziel, Remiel

Eating disorders: Anael, Isda, Uzziel

Ecology: Orifiel, Sandalphon

Education: Jophiel

Efficiency: Adnachiel, Caliel

Emotional healing: Balthiel, Chamuel, Gabriel, Lahabiel, Uriel

Emotions (controlling): Amitiel, Aniel, Gabriel, Ieiazel, Jophiel, Melahel, Muriel

Empathy: Vasariah

Employment: Anael, Uriel

Empowerment: Adnachiel, Raguel

Encouragement: Caliel, Jophiel, Metatron, Michael, Verchiel

Energy: Adnachiel, Gabriel, Michael, Raphael, Raziel, Yerathel

Enlightenment: Barbelo, Bath Kol, Jophiel, Raphael

Enthusiasm (*See* Optimism): Lauviah

Environment: Ariel, Uriel

Evil (to ward off): Ambriel

Evil Eye (preventing): Ambriel, Rahmiel, Sariel

Examination success: Achaiah, Mahasiah

Excellence: Lecabel

Exorcism: Haamiah, Mebahel, Yerathel

Faith (to encourage): Abadiel, Adnachiel, Michael, Raguel, Raphael, Uzziel

Family: Chamuel, Chavakhiah, Gabriel, Haaiah, Hanael, Jeliel, Raguel, Verchiel

Fertility: Abariel, Akriel, Anahita, Armisael, Borachiel, Gabriel, Isda, Jeliel, Omael, Samandriel

Fidelity: Chavakhiah, Iezalel

Flexibility: Raziel

Forgetfulness: Ansiel, Gabriel, Michael, Pathiel, Purah

Forgiveness: Adnachiel, Anael, Balthiel, Chamuel, Hariel, Jeremiel, Uzziel, Vasariah, Zadkiel, Zaphkiel

Freedom: Adnachiel, Barbelo, Gabriel, Reiyel

Friendship: Amnediel, Anael, Cambiel, Charmeine, Mebahel, Verchiel

Fulfillment: Omael

Gardening: Ariel, Omael, Uriel

Generosity: Sachiel, Sitael, Yeiayel, Zadkiel

Good fortune: Barchiel, Gabriel, Lelahel, Poiel, Zadkiel

Grace: Bath Kol, Hanael, Lahabiel, Raphael

Gratitude: Adnachiel, Cahatel, Gabriel, Melahel, Ooniemme, Paschar

Grief: Azrael, Raphael

Grounding: Gabriel, Isda

Guidance: Caliel, Gabriel, Raphael, Sariel

Guilt: Isda, Vasariah

Happiness (*See also* Joy): Barchiel, Eiael, Hanael, Lauviah, Lelahel, Nilaihah, Raphael

Harmony (between people): Cassiel, Gavreel, Haamiah, Hanael, Haziel, Jeliel, Lehahiah, Raguel, Raphael, Remiel, Sahaqiel, Uriel, Zuriel

Harvest: Omael

Hatred (to eliminate): Gabriel

Healing: Ariel, Gabriel, Harahel, Melahel, Melchizedek, Michael, Raphael, Sariel, Seheiah, Suriel, Uriel, Vehuiah, Zadkiel

Healing (children): Raphael, Zachariel

Health (good): Lelahel, Melahel, Raphael, Suriel, Zuriel

Health (mental): Rehael, Zuriel

Heartbreak (recovery from): Chamuel

Home: Barchiel, Cahatel, Iezalel, Uriel

Honesty: Adnachiel, Caliel, Haheuiah, Sitael, Vasariah, Yehuiah

Hope: Adnachiel, Anael, Perpetiel, Sariel

House (to buy): Uriel

Humanitarianism (*See also* Compassion, Forgiveness, Friendship, *and* Generosity): Mebahel

Humility: Rehael

Humor: Barchiel

Ideas (new): Aniel

Impulsiveness: Adnachiel, Caliel

Independence: Adnachiel

Inheritance: Chavakhiah

Initiative: Elemiah

Injury (healing mental and physical): Alimon, Michael, Raphael, Zuriel

Inner peace: Anael, Gavreel, Uriel

Inner strength: Ariel

Innocence: Aladiah

Insecurity: Balthiel

Insight: Hariel, Lalahel, Raziel

Insomnia: Hahaiah, Uriel

Inspiration: Caliel, Jophiel, Metatron

Integrity: Caliel, Haamiah

Intellect: Adnachiel, Asaliah, Barman, Cambiel, Lecabel, Leuviah, Uriel, Zachariel

Intimacy (*See also* **Love** *and* **Passion**): Isda, Pahaliah

Intuition (*See* **Divination**): Adnachiel, Amitiel, Lauviah

Inventions: Hariel, Lecabel

Jealousy (**to release**): Ariel, Balthiel, Barbelo, Gabriel, Uriel

Joy (*See also* **Happiness**): Caliel, Chamuel, Gabriel, Omael, Zadkiel

Judgement: Anael, Balthiel, Lahabiel, Raziel

Justice: Caliel, Chamuel, Lehahiah, Raguel, Rehael, Soterasiel

Karma: Aladiah, Aniel, Caliel, Cassiel, Halaliel, Lahabiel, Metatron, Zadkiel

Kindness: Haamiah, Hael, Lauviah, Vasariah

Knowledge (*See also* **Learning** *and* **Wisdom**): Adnachiel, Asaliah, Hamaliel, Jophiel, Raphael, Raziel, Sariel, Uriel

Languages, foreign: Mahasiah

Laws (**respect of**): Vasariah

Leadership: Gabriel, Hekamiah, Metatron, Vehuiah

Learning (*See also* **Knowledge** *and* **Wisdom**): Dina, Mahasiah, Nelkhael, Raziel

Legal concerns: Chamuel, Sachiel, Zadkiel

Liberty: Jeremiel, Metatron, Michael, Terathel

Limiting beliefs (**eliminating**): Metatron, Raziel

Listen (to others): Rehael

Loneliness: Chamuel

Longevity: Seheiah

Lost items: Chamuel, Michael, Rochel, Zadkiel

Love: Adriel, Amnediel, Anael, Ardifiel, Asmodel, Atliel, Balthiel, Barbelo, Chamuel, Charmeine, Darachiel, Donquel, Ergediel, Gabriel, Geliel, Haamiah, Hagiel, Hanael, Jeliel, Jophiel, Machidiel, Michael, Miniel, Muriel, Nilaihah, Rachiel, Raguel, Rahmiel, Raphael, Requiel, Sandalphon, Theliel, Uzziel, Verchiel, Zaphkiel

Loyalty: Chavakhiah, Hekamiah, Raphael, Yehuiah

Lucidity: Hakamiah, Lecabel

Luck, good: Barchiel

Magic: Ariel, Lahabiel, Raziel, Uriel

Manifestation (*See* Abundance, Money, *and* Wealth): Ariel, Bath Kol, Cambiel, Hanael, Lahabiel, Raziel, Uriel, Uzziel

Marriage (harmonious): Amnixiel, Chamuel, Gabriel, Haniel

Mediation: Jeliel

Meditation: Gabriel, Hahaiah, Iahhel, Raguel, Raphael, Raziel, Reiyel

Memories, happy: Iezalel

Memory: Leuviah, Mupiel, Vasariah, Zachariel, Zadkiel

Mercy: Gabriel, Jeremiel, Rahmiel, Uzziel

Messages: Gabriel

Mindfulness: Adnachiel, Chamuel, Melahel, Paschar

Miracle: Metatron, Michael, Uriel

Mistakes (correcting): Mahasiah

Moderation: Baglis

Modesty: Vasariah

Money (*See* Manifestation *and* Wealth): Ariel, Asmodel, Barchiel, Haniel, Jeremiel, Raziel, Sachiel, Uriel, Zadkiel

Morality: Hariel, Pahaliah

Motivation: Metatron, Michael, Verchiel

Music: Gabriel, Ieiazel, Israfil, Sandalphon, Uriel

Natural phenomena: Uriel

Negativity (warding off): Ambriel, Iahel, Jophiel

Negotiation: Haaiah, Sitael

Nervousness: Jophiel

Nourishment: Isda

Obedience: Lehahiah, Mitzrael

Obsession (controlling): Michael

Opportunity: Ambriel, Lahabiel

Optimism (*See* Enthusiasm): Adnachiel, Elemiah, Yerathel

Organization: Haaiah

Overeating (to stop): Raphael, Uzziel

Pain: Anael

Passion (to invoke): Adnachiel, Machidiel, Miniel

Passion (to control strong): Ieiazel

Past lives (to recall): Iahel, Leuviah

Patience: Achaiah, Asmodel, Bath Kol, Cassiel, Gabriel, Haamiah, Hamaliel, Leuviah, Omael

Peace: Balthiel, Barbelo, Cassiel, Chamuel, Chavakhiah, Gabriel, Gavreel, Lehahiah, Melchizedek, Nith-Maiah, Raguel, Raziel, Remiel, Uriel, Valoel, Zaphkiel

Persistence: Ariel, Perpetiel, Raguel, Samael

Persuasion: Jeliel

Philanthropy: Yeiayel

Philosophy: Mebahiah, Metatron, Raphael, Uriel

Planning: Lecabel, Sitael, Vasariah

Plant life: Orifiel, Sandalphon

Politeness: Haamiah

Politics: Sachiel

Positive attitude: Hahaiah, Yerathel

Power: Lahabiel, Metatron, Raphael, Raziel

Prayer: Guardian angel, Akatriel, Gabriel, Melchizedek, Metatron, Michael, Raphael, Salaphiel, Sandalphon, Sizouze

Pregnancy (protection during): Armisael, Avartiel, Badpatiel, Gabriel, Lailah, Omael, Sandalphon, Zuriel

Premonition: Seheiah

Problem solving: Achaiah, Raziel, Zachariel

Procrastination (overcoming): Adnachiel, Michael

Property: Adriel, Suriel

Prophecy: Jeremiel

Prosperity: Anauel, Ariel, Barbelo, Cambiel, Metatron, Raphael, Raziel, Remiel, Sachiel, Uriel, Zadkiel

Protection: Ambriel, Amitiel, Gabriel, guardian angel, Haheuiah, Lahabiel, Melahel, Michael, Raphael, Samael, Seheiah, Sidriel, Suriel, Uriel

Psychic attack (to ward off): Amitiel, Michael

Psychic skills (to develop): Amael, Azrael, Colopatiron, Gabriel, Hahaiah, Hanael, Jeremiel, Paschar, Raziel, Remiel

Punishment (suitable): Hutriel

Purification: Barbelo, Gabriel, Hariel, Michael, Raphael, Tahariel, Uriel

Purpose in life: Adnachiel, Chamuel, Gabriel, Metatron, Michael, Raziel, Uriel, Zadkiel

Reassurance: Raphael

Receptivity: Rehael

Recognition: Anael

Reconciliation: Chavakhiah

Regeneration: Rehael

Reincarnation (*See also* Death): Azrael, Leuviah

Relationships: Chamuel, Hanael, Isda, Jeliel

Relaxation: Asmodel

Repentance: Michael, Penuel, Raphael, Shepherd

Reputation (good): Yeiayel

Responsibility: Ambriel, Gabriel, Metatron, Omael

Rituals: Haamiah

Sadness (overcoming): Lauviah

Science: Cambiel, Hamaliel, Hariel, Raphael

Secrets: Achaiah, Haaiah, Jeremiel. Satarel

Security: Raphael

Self-esteem: Adnachiel, Anael, Balthiel, Iahel, Jehudiel, Metatron, Michael

Self-love: Chamuel, Gabriel, Michael

Sensitivity: Adnachiel, Gabriel, Rehael, Umabel

Serenity: Asmodel, Cassiel

Sexuality: Balthiel, Haamiah, Isda, Pahaliah

Sincerity: Haheuiah

Sleep (to encourage): Gabriel, Lauviah, Raphael

Solitude: Hahaiah, Nith-Haiah

Solutions (to problems): Jeliel, Michael, Urieliel

Soul connection: Gabriel, Raziel

Soul mate: Chamuel, Hanael

Soul purpose: Michael

Spirituality: Asmodel, Balthiel, Elemiah, Haamiah, Hariel, Jegudiel, Melchizedek, Micah, Pahaliah, Sachiel, Sandalphon

Spontaneity: Caliel

Stability: Raphael, Raziel

Starting again: Aladiah

Strength: Camael, Gabriel, Metatron, Michael, Raphael, Raziel

Stress: Raphael

Study: Akriel, Asaliah, Cambiel, Caliel, Hamaliel, Harahel, Iahhel, Jophiel, Mahasiah, Metatron, Michael, Nelkhael, Pallas, Raphael, Uriel, Vesta, Zachariel, Zadkiel

Success: Gazriel, Lauviah, Malkiel, Perpetiel, Vehuiah, Verchiel

Sympathy: Michael

Talents: Adnachiel, Lecabel

Teaching: Nelkhael

Tears: Sandalphon

Technology: Nelkhael

Temperance: Cassiel

Temptation (avoiding): Aladiah

Transcendence: Haamiah

Transformation: Cambiel, Raziel

Transition: Raziel, Remiel

Travel: Elemiah, Orifiel, Raphael, Yeiayel

Trust: Adnachiel, Amitiel, Barbelo, Chavakhiah, Gabriel, Isda, Michael, Raguel, Raphael, Raziel, Tezalel

Truth: Achaiah, Adnachiel, Amitiel, Caliel, Gabriel, Jophiel, Menadel, Michael, Raphael, Raziel, Rehael, Reiyel

Understanding: Lelahel, Rehael

Universal love: Chamuel, Hekamiah, Nith-Maiah, Reiyel

Validation: Adnachiel

Vision: Gabriel, Iaoel, Michael

Vitality: Isda, Raphael

Vocation: Menadel

Wealth, material (*See* Abundance, Manifestation, *and* Wealth): Cahetel

Weather: Uriel, Zaphkiel

Weight loss: Anael, Iahel, Isda, Raphael

Willpower: Gabriel, Menadel

Wisdom (*See also* Knowledge): Chavakhiah, Damabiah, Gabriel, Jeliel, Melchizedek, Metatron, Nith-Haiah, Raphael, Raziel, Sagnessagiel, Seheiah, Sophia, Uriel, Vasariah, Zadkiel (for spiritual wisdom), Zagzagel

Work: Cahetel, Menadel

Worry (eliminating): Adnachiel, Caliel, Lauviah, Michael

Bibliography

Adey, Oliver. "The Afghan walk, the benefits of a regenerating walk." Get to Text website, October 9, 2020. https://gettotext.com /the-afghan-walk-the-benefits-of-a-regenerating-walk/.

Adler, Mortimer J. *The Angels and Us*. New York: Macmillan Publishing Co, 1982.

Amber, Reuben. *Color Therapy: Healing with Color*. Santa Fe: Aurora Press, 1983.

Barrett, Francis. *The Magus*. Wellingborough, UK: The Aquarian Press, 1989. Originally published in 1801 by Lackington, Alley, and Company (London).

Barth, Karl. *Church Dogmatics*. Vol. 3, part 3. Translated by G. W. Bromiley and R. J. Ehrlich. Edinburgh: T & T Clark, 1960.

BBC News. "More than 900 cars 'pay-it forward' in random act of drive-through kindness." December 9, 2020. https://www.bbc .com/news/world-us-canada-55254082.

Bloom, Harold. *Omens of Millennium: The Gnosis of Angels, Dreams, and Resurrection*. New York: Riverhead Books, 1997.

Bullinger, E. W. *The Witness of the Stars*. London: Lamp Press, 1893. (This is an extremely rare book; digital copies are available from many sources online.)

Bunson, Matthew. *Angels A to Z*. New York: Crown Trade Paperbacks, 1996.

Burke, Peter. *The Polymath: A Cultural History from Leonardo da Vinci to Susan Sontag*. New Haven, CT: Yale University Press, 2020.

Burnham, Sophy. *A Book of Angels: Reflections on Angels Past and Present, and True Stories of How They Touch Our Lives*. New York: Ballantine Books, 1990.

Castle, Tony, ed. *The Way of Prayer*. New York: Crossroad Publishing, 1995.

Chardin, Pierre Teilhard. *The Heart of Matter*. London: William Collins Sons & Co., 1978.

Chase, Steven. *Angelic Spirituality: Medieval Perspectives on the Ways of Angels*. Mahwah, NJ: Paulist Press, 2002.

Collins, Leah. "Job unhappiness is at a staggering all-time high, according to Gallup," *CNBC News*, August 12, 2022. https://www.cnbc.com/2022/08/12/job-unhappiness-is-at-a-staggering-all-time-high-according-to-gallup.html.

Davidson, Gustav. *A Dictionary of Angels Including the Fallen Angels*. New York: The Free Press, 1967.

Emmons, Robert A. *Thanks! How the New Science of Gratitude Can Make You Happier*. New York: Houghton Mifflin Company, 2007.

———. *The Little Book of Gratitude: Create a Life of Happiness and Wellbeing by Giving Thanks*. London: Octopus Publishing Group Limited, 2016.

Emmons, Robert A., and Michael E. McCullough. "Counting Blessings Versus Burdens: An Experimental Investigation of Gratitude and Subjective Well-Being in Daily Life." *Journal of Personality*

and Social Psychology 84, no. 2 (2003). https://greatergood
.berkeley.edu/pdfs/GratitudePDFs/6Emmons-BlessingsBurdens
.pdf.

Emoto, Masaru. *Messages from Water and the Universe*. Carlsbad,
CA: Hay House, 2010.

Garrett, Susan R. *No Ordinary Angel: Celestial Spirits and Christian
Claims About Jesus*. New Haven, CT: Yale University Press, 2008.

George, Leonard. *Alternative Realities: The Paranormal, the Mystic
and the Transcendent in Human Experience*. New York: Facts on
File, 1995.

Gilbert, Josiah Hotchkiss. *Dictionary of Burning Words of Brilliant
Writers*. New York: W. B. Ketcham, 1895.

Ginzberg, Louis. *The Legends of the Jews*. Volume 1. Philadelphia:
The Jewish Publication Society, 1954.

Graham, Billy. *Angels: God's Secret Agents*. Dallas: Word Publishing,
1975.

Harvard Health. "Benefits of Mindfulness," *HelpGuide.org*, February
23, 2023. https://www.helpguide.org/harvard/benefits
-of-mindfulness.htm.

Kahneman, Daniel, and Angus Deaton. "High income improves
evaluation of life but not emotional well-being." *Proceedings of the
National Academy of Science*, August 4, 2010. https://www.pnas
.org/doi/10.1073/pnas.1011492107.

Katzir, Shaul. *The Beginnings of Piezoelectricity: A Study in Mundane
Physics*. Dordrecht, Netherlands: Springer, 2006.

Keck, David. *Angels and Angelology in the Middle Ages*. New York:
Oxford University Press, 1998.

Mandela, Nelson. *Nelson Mandela: In His Own Words*. New York:
Little, Brown & Co., 2003.

Misuhashi, Yukari. *Ikigai: Giving Every Day Meaning and Joy*. London: Octopus Publishing Group, 2018.

Nightingale, Earl. *This is Earl Nightingale*. Garden City, NY: Doubleday & Company, 1969.

Peale, Norman Vincent. *The Power of Positive Thinking*. New York: Prentice-Hall, 1952.

Peterson, Christopher. *A Primer in Positive Psychology*. New York: Oxford University Press, 2006.

Quote Investigator. "He Has Achieved Success Who Has Lived Well, Laughed Often and Loved Much." June 26, 2012. https://quoteinvestigator.com/2012/06/26/define-success/.

Ronner, John. *Know Your Angels: The Angel Almanac with Biographies of 100 Prominent Angels in Legend and Folklore, and Much More*. Murfreesboro, TN: Mamre Press, 1993.

Scholem, Gershom, ed. *Zohar, the Book of Splendor: Basic Readings from the Kabbalah*. New York: Schocken Books/Random House, 1995.

Siegle, Steve. "The art of kindness." *Speaking of Health* (blog), Mayo Clinic Health System, May 29, 2020. https://www.mayoclinichealthsystem.org/hometown-health/speaking-of-health/the-art-of-kindness.

Smith, Delia. *You Matter: The Human Solution*. London: Mensch Publishing, 2022.

Spitzer, Toba. *God Is Here: Reimagining the Divine*. New York: St. Martin's Essentials, 2022.

Stiegler, Édouard. *Régénération par la marche afghane*. Paris: Guy Tredaniel, 1981.

Streets, Annabel. *52 Ways to Walk*. London: Bloomsbury Publishing, 2022.

Von Hochheim, Eckhart. "Sermon Nine." In *The Reading and Preaching of the Scriptures in the Worship of the Christian Church V*, edited by Hughes Oliphant Old. Grand Rapids, MI: Wm. B. Eerdmans Publishing Company, 1998.

Watkins, Philip C. *Gratitude and the Good Life: Toward a Psychology of Appreciation*. New York: Springer Publishing, 2014.

Webster, Richard. *Angels for Beginners*. Woodbury, MN: Llewellyn Publications, 2017.

———. *Archangels: How to Invoke & Work with Angelic Messengers*. Woodbury, MN: Llewellyn Publications, 2022.

———. *Communicating with the Archangel Gabriel for Inspiration & Reconciliation*. Woodbury, MN: Llewellyn Publications, 2005.

———. *Communicating with the Archangel Michael for Guidance & Protection*. St. Paul, MN: Llewellyn Publications, 2004.

———. *Communicating with the Archangel Raphael for Healing & Creativity*. St. Paul, MN: Llewellyn Publications, 2005.

———. *Communicating with the Archangel Uriel for Transformation & Tranquility*. Woodbury, MN: Llewellyn Publications, 2005.

———. *Encyclopedia of Angels*. Woodbury, MN: Llewellyn Publications, 2009.

———. *Guardian Angels: How to Contact & Work with Angelic Protectors*. Woodbury, MN: Llewellyn Publications, 2022.

———. *Praying with Angels*. Woodbury, MN: Llewellyn Publications, 2007.

———. *Spirit Guides & Angel Guardians*. St. Paul, MN: Llewellyn Publications, 1998.

Woodward, Mary Ann. *Edgar Cayce's Story of Karma: God's Book of Remembrance*. New York: Coward-McCann Books, 1971.

To Write to the Author

If you wish to contact the author or would like more information about this book, please write to the author in care of Llewellyn Worldwide Ltd. and we will forward your request. Both the author and publisher appreciate hearing from you and learning of your enjoyment of this book and how it has helped you. Llewellyn Worldwide Ltd. cannot guarantee that every letter written to the author can be answered, but all will be forwarded. Please write to:

Richard Webster
℅ Llewellyn Worldwide
2143 Wooddale Drive
Woodbury, MN 55125-2989
Please enclose a self-addressed stamped envelope for reply,
or $1.00 to cover costs. If outside the U.S.A., enclose
an international postal reply coupon.

Many of Llewellyn's authors have websites with additional information and resources. For more information, please visit our website at http://www.llewellyn.com.